Contents

Getting along

Lesson A Vocabulary House rules

A Circle the best option to complete the house rules.

Rules for dormitory living

1. If a problem comes **up / over / off**, please call the building manager.
2. If you make a mess, clean it **up / to / over**.
3. If you see trash on the floor, pick it **on / over / up** and throw it away.
4. When you leave your room, be sure to turn **over / off / back** the lights.
5. Talk quietly in the hallways so you don't wake people **over / forward / up**.
6. If you have friends **with / over / out**, they must leave the building by 11:00 p.m.

B Complete the two parts of the conversation with the expressions in the boxes.

come up with	go over	✔ look forward to	put off	wake up

Ji Ning I never look forward to our house meetings. But I guess tonight's meeting is important. There are so many things we need to _____ .

Clara I agree. Things haven't been going well lately. We should have had the meeting weeks ago. I don't know why we _____ it _____ so many times.

Ji Ning Well, part of the problem is Jasmina. When she's here, all she does is sleep. I try to be quiet because I don't want to _____ her _____ , but it's not really possible to have a life when someone next door is sleeping all the time.

Clara Well, we have to _____ a plan. If we don't, we'll be fighting all the time.

clean up	give back	give up	have over	put up with	run out of

Jasmina Sorry I'm late, guys. I've been working overtime – again. I wish I could _____ my job _____ , but you know how much I need the money.

Ji Ning OK, so let's start our meeting. So, we were just saying that we don't want to have to be quiet all afternoon just because you're sleeping. We _____ it because we know you're tired, but . . .

Jasmina OK, OK. I get it. But can I say something? Clara, you need to do the dishes more often. I hate it when we _____ clean plates and glasses. It happens all the time. Everyone loves to _____ friends _____ , but you have to _____ afterwards.

Clara You're absolutely right. Oh, before I forget, Jasmina, could you _____ my DVD _____ ? You know, the one you borrowed last week?

Jasmina Of course. I'll get it right now.

VIEWPOINT

WORKBOOK 1B

MICHAEL MCCARTHY

JEANNE MCCARTEN

HELEN SANDIFORD

CAMBRIDGE
UNIVERSITY PRESS

CAMBRIDGE
UNIVERSITY PRESS

University Printing House, Cambridge CB2 8BS, United Kingdom

One Liberty Plaza, 20th Floor, New York, NY 10006, USA

477 Williamstown Road, Port Melbourne, VIC 3207, Australia

314-321, 3rd Floor, Plot 3, Splendor Forum, Jasola District Centre, New Delhi – 110025, India

79 Anson Road, #06–04/06, Singapore 079906

Cambridge University Press is part of the University of Cambridge.

It furthers the University's mission by disseminating knowledge in the pursuit of education, learning and research at the highest international levels of excellence.

www.cambridge.org
Information on this title: www.cambridge.org/9781107602793

First published 2012

Printed in Italy by Rotolito S.p.A.

A catalogue record for this publication is available from the British Library

ISBN 978-0-521-13186-5 Student's Book 1
ISBN 978-1-107-60151-2 Student's Book 1A
ISBN 978-1-107-60152-9 Student's Book 1B
ISBN 978-1-107-60277-9 Workbook 1
ISBN 978-1-107-60278-6 Workbook 1A
ISBN 978-1-107-60279-3 Workbook 1B
ISBN 978-1-107-60153-6 Teacher's Edition 1
ISBN 978-1-107-63988-1 Classroom Audio 1
ISBN 978-1-107-62978-3 Classware 1

Cambridge University Press has no responsibility for the persistence or accuracy of URLs for external or third-party internet websites referred to in this publication, and does not guarantee that any content on such websites is, or will remain, accurate or appropriate. Information regarding prices, travel timetables, and other factual information given in this work is correct at the time of first printing but Cambridge University Press does not guarantee the accuracy of such information thereafter.

Cover and interior design: Page 2, LLC
Layout/design services and photo research: Cenveo Publisher Services/Nesbitt Graphics, Inc.
Audio production: New York Audio Productions

Lesson A Grammar Using phrasal verbs

A **Unscramble the words in parentheses to complete the house rules.**

1. When you have to get up early, try not to _____ .
   (the entire household / up / wake)

2. When you _____ , be considerate and don't make too much
   noise. (friends / over / have)

3. _____ on time for house meetings. (up / show)

4. If we _____ , replace it quickly. (out / run / something / of)

5. If you are the last one to watch TV, _____ before you go to bed. (it / turn / off)

6. If you borrow things from your roommates, don't forget to _____ . (back / them / give)

7. Let's _____ the bills together so everyone knows how much to pay. (go / over)

8. If you disagree, try to _____ without arguing. (with / up / come / solutions)

B **Complete the anecdote with the words in parentheses. Write them in the correct order and place. Sometimes more than one answer is possible.**

> My roommate's just so annoying – she wakes me ^up every morning. (up) She's always running cash
> and forgets to pay the bills. (of / out) She never shows when we have a meeting with the building
> manager. (up) Then, whenever she cooks, she always puts cleaning her mess. (off / up) Sometimes
> she won't do a thing for days! Will this work? (out) I'd love to come up a solution to this problem, but
> I don't think that I can put with her bad habits any longer! (with / up)

About you

C **Complete B's responses with a correct form of the phrasal verb that A uses. Add the pronouns *them* or *it*. Then answer the questions with your own ideas.**

1. *A* Do you usually put up with your friends' annoying habits?

   B I generally <u>put up with them</u> – as long as they put up with mine!

   _____

2. *A* Do you often put off chores?

   B Yeah, I hate doing chores. I _____ as long as I can.

   _____

3. *A* How do you get over an argument with friends or family?

   B Oh, I usually figure out a way to _____ . You know, sometimes humor helps.

   _____

4. *A* How likely are you to give up a bad habit when someone is constantly commenting on it?

   B Well, it depends! If it's a really bad habit, I'll try to _____ .

   _____

Lesson B Grammar Describing experiences

A Circle the correct form of the verbs to complete the childhood memory.

As an only child, my mother had always wanted siblings **to play / playing** with. When she and my father got married, they agreed it was important **to have / having** more than one child. So they had six kids! Things weren't always easy, though. For example, there was never anywhere quiet **for / to** sit in our house. But I always had fun **to hang out / hanging out** with my older sisters.

My brother was the only boy, so he was often bored **to play / playing** with girls all the time. And you know, I think he was a bit lonely **to be / being** surrounded by so many girls. But mostly, we had no problem **to grow up / growing up** in such a big family, and we're all still very close.

B Complete the conversations with a correct form of the verbs given. Sometimes more than one answer is possible.

1. *A* You were an only child, right? Weren't you bored __playing__ (play) by yourself all the time?
    B Sometimes. But there were a lot of families in my building, so there was always a neighbor's apartment _____ (go) to.

2. *A* Was it tough _____ (grow up) with so many kids in the house? Did you argue a lot?
    B No, not really. We had no problem _____ (get along). There weren't enough toys _____ (play) with, so we learned that it was important _____ (share).

3. *A* My dad worked a lot when I was a kid. When he came home from the office, he was always really tired and it was hard for him _____ (find) any time for me.
    B So do you think you had problems _____ (connect) with him?
    A Well, yeah. My mother had lots of time _____ (spend) with me, but I think it was difficult for her _____ (be) almost like a single mom.

4. *A* Do you think it's worth _____ (wait) until you're like 38 to have children?
    B Oh, it depends. My parents had fun _____ (travel) before they had me. But I had kids when I was pretty young and had no trouble _____ (raise) them. It's impossible _____ (say) what's better.

About you

C Answer the questions with information that is true for you.

1. Do you think that it's important for children to have siblings? Why or why not?

    _____

    _____

2. Who did you play with when you were growing up? What did you play?

    _____

    _____

3. When you were growing up which family members did you have problems getting along with? Who did you have no trouble getting along with? Why?

    _____

    _____

Lesson C Conversation strategies

A **Choose the appropriate responses to complete the conversation.**

Emma Did I tell you I moved out of my parents' house last week?

Jayne Really? That's wonderful! I mean, it must be _____ .

a. great having your own place   b. difficult living on your own

Emma Yeah, I couldn't wait. I'm not saying _____ . It's just that I was ready, you know?

a. I hated living with my parents   b. I want to live with my parents

Jayne Yeah. And now you can have people over! What I mean is, _____ .

a. you can come over to see me   b. you'll have fun hanging out with friends

Emma Yeah, but to tell you the truth, I'm just a little nervous about cooking for myself every day.
I mean _____ .

a. I never cooked much at home   b. I cook all the time

Jayne Oh, it's not even worth worrying about. What I'm saying is, you'll _____ .

a. have problems with it   b. be fine. It's no big deal

B **Complete the conversations with the sentences in the box. There is one extra sentence.**

> To tell you the truth, my friends gave the best advice.
> I have to say, it's much easier financially.
> Well, I'm an only child, and to be honest, it was lonely.
> Honestly, parents are more likely to tell you what you need to hear.

1. *A* I think it's good for kids to grow up in big families. You know what I mean?

   B I don't know. I grew up in a big family, and I have to say, it's not always easy competing for your parents' attention.

   A _____

2. *A* I read online that kids take more advice from their friends than from their parents.

   B I suppose that's true. I always went to my friends for advice, which wasn't always a good idea.

   _____

3. *A* This is so embarrassing! I graduated two years ago, and I'm still living at home.

   B Yeah, but lots of people our age still live at home. _____

C **Complete the conversation with the sentences below. Write the letters a–e.**

Samia My older brother still lives at home, and my parents pay for everything!
It's just not fair. ____

Marek Yeah, that seems pretty unfair. ____

Samia I've never asked my parents for anything. ____

Marek Yeah. The thing is it could cause problems between you and your brother. ____

Samia You're right. You know what? I'm going to talk to him about it tonight. ____

> a. I don't mean that they wouldn't help me if I asked, but I try to be independent.
> b. I have to say, it's tough if your parents are giving your brother more support than you.
> c. What I mean is *I* pay for everything myself, and I think he should too, to be honest.
> d. I mean, if I don't say anything, the problem will only get worse.
> e. And quite frankly, you don't want money problems stopping you from getting along.

Lesson D Reading The perfect roommate?

A Prepare What is your idea of a perfect roommate? Write four ideas. Then scan the article to see if any of your ideas are mentioned.

How to get rid of the PERFECT ROOMMATE

1   So you've moved out of your parents' house for the first time, and if you're like most young people on a tight budget, chances are that you probably have a roommate. But what's your roommate like? Does he or she consult you before having friends over? Or clean up all the mess in the apartment? That's obnoxious! If a problem comes up, does your roommate come up with an idea for solving it? Well, don't worry. There's a way to deal with that.

2   Are you seeing other eccentric behavior, too – with the chores, for example? Does your roommate do them every day and never put them off? This sets a bad example for everyone! To make things worse, your roommate is probably never short of money (that's just not normal if you're a student, right?) and always pays the bills on time. When you and your friends from college go out, your roommate would never tag along with you – not without an invitation. Right? Don't you think that's a little weird?

3   If any of this sounds like your roommate, then you have one who's just too perfect – and that's no good! It's tough living with someone you can't argue with and who doesn't complain. That's just no fun! You need to get rid of this roommate, and you shouldn't put it off. If you let this person stay too long, these bad habits could start to rub off on you.

4   But all is not lost. If you follow these suggestions, you'll have no trouble getting your roommate off your back.

5   • Set your alarm for 5:00 a.m., and turn it off every five minutes until you're ready to get up for class – two hours later.

   • Tell your roommate you'll take out the trash, and then never get around to it.

   • Make it impossible for your roommate to have time alone with friends. When he or she has friends over, talk loudly on your cell phone and refuse to leave the room until you drive them away.

   • Come up with great ideas for meals, but then don't make them. Forget to go to the supermarket, and then suggest ordering a pizza – again. When the pizza delivery guy comes, ask your roommate – who always has money – to pay. You have a student loan to pay off and other things to worry about, right?

   • Make sure your roommate always has chores to do and never has any free time. When he or she's not looking, undo the chores he or she just did. For example, collect bottles and cans in your closet. Fill the empty recycling bin with them right after your roommate has taken out the recycling.

   • Run out of cash right before it's time to pay the rent. Borrow money from your roommate, and then pay it back – $5 at a time.

   • Let your roommate down regularly. For example, invite him or her to a friend's party, but don't give him or her the address. Then disappear all day and come home late, talking about the fabulous time you had.

6   These techniques should help you get rid of your perfect roommate forever. After all, you don't want someone to help with the chores. Quite frankly, you don't want anyone to do the chores. You want to put them off as long as you can. I mean, why clean up a mess when you could be studying. Right?

B Read for style **Check (✔) the true statements about the article.**

☐ 1. It is aimed at families who don't get along.
☐ 2. It has advice on getting along with roommates.
☐ 3. It says the opposite of what is true.

☐ 4. It is written for parents.
☐ 5. It is not a serious article.
☐ 6. It is useful advice.

C Understanding reference **Find the sentences in the article. What do the underlined words refer to?**

1. <u>That's</u> obnoxious! (para. 1) _____

2. . . . does your roommate come up with an idea for solving <u>it</u>? (para. 1) _____

3. Does your roommate do <u>them</u> every day and never put <u>them</u> off? (para. 2) _____

4. <u>This</u> sets a bad example for everyone! (para. 2) _____

5. Don't you think <u>that's</u> a little weird? (para. 2) _____

6. <u>That's</u> just no fun! (para. 3) _____

7. . . . and refuse to leave the room until you drive <u>them</u> away. (para. 5) _____

8. Fill the empty recycling bin with <u>them</u> . . . (para. 5) _____

D Read for detail **Find these sentences in the article. What do they mean? Check (✔) a or b.**

1. This sets a bad example for everyone! (para. 2)
   ☐ a. Your roommate should always put off doing chores, because everyone does.
   ☐ b. If other people start behaving the same way as your roommate, you'll have to as well.

2. It's tough living with someone you can't argue with and who doesn't complain. (para. 3)
   ☐ a. Your roommate is just too nice. You want a *normal* roommate.
   ☐ b. Your roommate is so lazy, it's driving you crazy!

3. If you let this person stay too long, these bad habits could start to rub off on you. (para. 3)
   ☐ a. Over time, this person's good behavior will force you to be a better roommate.
   ☐ b. Over time, this person's bad habits will make all your roommates behave badly.

E Focus on vocabulary **Find the expressions below in the article. Then complete the sentences with the expressions.**

be short of	get around to	let down
drive away	get off your back	tag along with

1. It's important for you to share the chores and the bills. You don't want to _____ your roommate _____ and end up living alone.

2. Let your roommate _____ you occasionally when you go out.

3. If your roommate doesn't _____ doing the dishes, it's not worth worrying about.

4. Be a good roommate: try not to _____ your roommate _____ . A promise is a promise!

5. It's impossible to _____ an annoying roommate _____ without hurting his or her feelings. If you have problems, talk them through. He or she will thank you for it!

6. Budget carefully. You don't want to _____ money, especially at the end of the month when there are bills to pay.

Writing An introduction to an essay

Essay question

A recent research paper states: "Children don't try to copy adults as much as we think – they're trying to be like other children." This implies that other children have a greater influence on a child than his or her parents. Do you agree or disagree with this statement?

A **Read the introductory paragraph to an essay. Underline the thesis statement.**

Most people agree that a child's personality is shaped by his or her environment. On the one hand, an important part of a child's environment is his or her parents and their parenting style. Children learn some important lessons from their parents. On the other hand, a child's need to get along in a group influences his or her behavior even more. In my opinion, what is most important in the end is the social behavior that children learn from their friends.

B **Rewrite the underlined part of each sentence with a *What* clause.**

1. <u>Children need</u> to fit in with one another.
   What children need is to fit in with one another.

2. <u>It is clear</u> that friends have the strongest influence on a child's personality.

3. <u>It is essential</u> to guide your child's choice of social groups.

4. <u>This means</u> that a child's parents are not as important as his or her friends.

5. <u>It is likely</u> that parents play a more insignificant role in their child's emotional development.

6. <u>Children perceive</u> that their friends are the people who are most like them.

C **Editing Correct the sentences. There is one error in each sentence.**

1. Is important to help your child choose his or her social groups wisely.

2. What means is that friends have a strong influence on a child.

3. Is clear that children aren't interested in becoming copies of their parents.

4. What implies is children teach one another to be social.

5. Is interesting that children almost always learn behavior from their friends.

D **Write an introduction to the essay question. Include a thesis statement. Then check your introduction for errors.**

Listening extra *Ask Alison!*

A Look at the list of complaints about people. Which of the complaints are problems for you? Give each complaint a number from 0 (not a problem) to 10 (a big problem) in the first column.

Common complaints about people	Me	The callers
a. He/She never returns your calls.	☐	☐
b. He/She is always late.	☐	☐
c. He/She never helps clean up after dinner.	☐	☐
d. He/She tags along without an invitation.	☐	☐
e. He/She takes up all your free time.	☐	☐
f. He/She is always borrowing money.	☐	☐

B ⬇ Listen to the call-in radio show. Number the complaints in Exercise A in the order you hear the callers mention them. There are two extra complaints.

C ⬇ Listen again. Are the sentences true or false? Write T or F. Correct the false sentences.

1. Mark orders in pizza or pasta for his brother. _____
2. Alison advises Mark to be direct with his brother. _____
3. Laura's problem is with her roommate. _____
4. Laura has tried to solve the problem. _____
5. Berto wants to spend more time with his girlfriend. _____
6. Alison advises Berto to plan regular date nights. _____

About you

D ⬇ Listen again. Do you agree or disagree with the advice? Write why or why not. Then write your own responses to the callers' complaints.

1. Advice for Mark: **agree / disagree**? _____

   My advice: _____

   _____

   _____

   _____

2. Advice for Laura: **agree / disagree**? _____

   My advice: _____

   _____

   _____

   _____

3. Advice for Berto: **agree / disagree**? _____

   My advice: _____

   _____

   _____

   _____

Now complete the *Unit 7 Progress chart* on page 100.

Food science

Unit 8

Lesson A Grammar Information focus

A Complete the sentences with a correct passive form of the verbs given.

1. With global warming, it _____is thought_____ (think) that harvests in some parts of the world _____ (will affect) by drought. As a result, crops that can survive in drier weather conditions _____ (must develop). Recently, crops that need less water _____ (have grown). In addition, these crops _____ (can grow) in poor soil with few nutrients.

2. In the future, it _____ (hope) that more food _____ (will sell) in the same areas where it _____ (produce). This would mean that crops _____ (will not transport) over long distances from farmer to consumer. It also means that less food _____ (would import).

B Rewrite each sentence in the paragraph in the passive without *they*.

Organic food is food that **they** grow without pesticides. **They** have practiced organic farming methods for thousands of years. It became less popular in the twentieth century as **they** invented more productive methods. **They** didn't consider organic farming effective, and **they** used more pesticides and other chemicals to increase crop yields and grow more food. More recently, however, **they** have reconsidered the value of organic farming, and **they** expect the market for organic food to grow in the future.

Organic food is food that is grown without pesticides.
_____
_____

C Rewrite the predictions in the passive. Start with the words given. Add *by* if necessary.

1. In countries that have food shortages, farmers are going to use improved farming methods.
   Improved farming methods _____ .

2. Engineers are going to build better greenhouses so we can have longer growing seasons.
   Supermarkets will sell less imported fruit in the future.
   Better greenhouses _____ . Less imported fruit _____ .

3. Supermarkets are going to encourage consumers to buy more food that is produced locally.
   They're no longer going to fly food halfway around the world.
   Consumers _____ . Food _____ .

Lesson B Vocabulary For your health

A Circle the correct option to label the picture.

5. brain / liver _____

1. digestive system / heart _____

6. muscles / teeth _____

7. heart / liver _____

2. liver / skin _____

8. digestive system / muscles _____

3. heart / muscles _____

4. bones / muscles _____

B Complete the sentences with the words in the box.

1. The _____ removes toxins and is part of your digestive system.
2. The _____ controls thought, memory, and feelings.
3. _____ produce movement in your body.
4. The _____ pumps blood around the body.
5. _____ covers your body and protects it from disease.
6. The _____ processes food so that it can be used by the body for energy.

| brain |
| digestive system |
| heart |
| liver |
| muscles |
| skin |

C Complete the excerpts from a presentation with the words in the box.

| blood pressure | digestive system | immune system | skin |
| bones | eyesight | metabolism | teeth |

Today I'd like to talk about "functional" foods. These are foods that are considered to have extra health benefits such as strengthening your _____ so that you can fight disease, or lowering your _____ , which is important for good heart health. Typically, "functional" foods have added nutrients. For example, calcium-fortified orange juice. As most people know, you need calcium to help prevent your _____ from breaking, and for healthy _____ and gums. . . .

. . . We'll move on and look at another product. Some yogurt manufacturers claim that the probiotics in their products help the stomach and _____ to process food better. Other studies have shown some low-fat yogurts can help increase your _____ and possibly lead to weight loss. . . .

. . . So, in the future, "functional" foods are going to become big business. We might even see cake mixes that help improve your _____ and help you see better at night. Or drinks that contain additives that can keep your _____ clear and healthy, and prevent it from aging so quickly.

Lesson B Grammar Describing causes and results

A **Circle the correct form of the verbs to complete the sentences.**

1. Using a lot of salt may cause your blood pressure **from rising** / **to rise**.
2. Eating too much sugar may make your immune system **work** / **to work** more slowly.
3. Paying attention to food labels enables you **make** / **to make** better choices.
4. Some people say you should let your body **tell** / **to tell** you what foods it needs.
5. Eating avocados may protect you **getting** / **from getting** heart disease.
6. Drinking a lot of water may allow you **to control** / **from controlling** your weight.
7. Chili peppers can keep you **to gain** / **from gaining** weight.

B **Complete the conversation with a correct form of the verbs given. Add *from* where necessary. Sometimes more than one answer is possible.**

A You know, my friend only eats raw food. It's supposed to prevent you _____ (age), and she says it keeps you _____ (have) problems with your digestive system.

B Isn't that because a raw-food diet enables you _____ (digest) food more quickly? So it helps you _____ (absorb) more nutrients?

A Yes, but I believe some foods are better cooked, like tomatoes. Cooking them lets the fiber _____ (break down), and it allows you _____ (get) more of the nutrients.

B Huh. Don't tomatoes protect you _____ (get) certain types of cancer, too?

A I don't know. I heard that they can help you _____ (control) your blood pressure.

B So they can make your blood pressure _____ (go down)?

A Well, I don't think they cause your blood pressure _____ (rise).

B I should eat more tomatoes. It looks like they could help me _____ (improve) my health!

C **Complete the article with the words in parentheses. Put the words in the correct order and form. Add *from* where necessary. If you can leave *from* out, write ( ). Sometimes more than one answer is possible.**

Here are our top tips for staying fit and feeling great

- Drinking lots of water can _____ (lose / help / you) weight. It increases your metabolism and can _____ (you / eat / stop) too much.

- Are you sleeping enough? Research has shown that sleeping at least seven or eight hours a night might _____ (protect / skin / age / your).

- Experts say breakfast is the most important meal of the day. One healthy breakfast food, cereal, might _____ (you / get / protect) heart disease. Add some blueberries to your cereal. They will _____ (concentrate / you / help).

- Exercise. Regular exercise is good for your heart, and it can _____ (get / you / keep) heart disease. Exercise, such as running or swimming, can _____ (keep / help / bones / your) stronger. Exercise also _____ (help / have / prevent / people) health problems later on in life.

Lesson C   Conversation strategies

A Complete the conversations with the best rhetorical questions in the box. Write the letters a–e. There is one extra question.

> a. I mean, can that even be good for you?   d. I mean, what was I thinking?
> b. I mean, where did you get that idea?   e. I mean, can't we just grow everything locally?
> c. Why are their vegetables so expensive?

1. *A* You never know where food comes from these days. Take apples, for instance. The apples I
   bought today are from the other side of the world! That can't be environmentally friendly. ___
   B I know. I just bought some stuff at the farmers' market. It's so much fresher than at the
   supermarket, but I spent a fortune. ___

2. *A* My best friend only eats raw vegetables. ___ Surely you need to eat protein and other stuff, too.
   B Oh, yeah. I tried a ten-day fast once, where you just drink juice. It was crazy! ___

B Circle the best expressions to complete what Lee says.

"So, yeah, I'm trying to improve my diet and avoid all those bad things that I
love eating! So **for instance, / take** instead of drinking soda, I've started making
smoothies. If you drink one every day, you're getting lots of good nutrients. I'm
also avoiding eating processed foods, **look at / such as** frozen dinners, which
probably have a lot of additives in them. It's not easy, though. I'm also
trying to find out more about the food I eat, **like / look at** does it contain
artificial colors, or where does it come from? I mean, **take / such as** fruit
and vegetables, **for example / take**. What kinds of pesticides have been
used on them? And **such as / look at** food packages – they make a lot of claims, but how do we
know what's true? Does low-fat really mean low-calorie, **for example / such as**?"

Lee

C Complete the conversation with the rhetorical questions below. Write the letters a–e in the
boxes in the conversation. There is one extra question. Then write expressions (*like, such as,* etc.)
to show where the speakers are giving examples. Sometimes more than one answer is possible.

> a. I mean, who wants soft bananas?   d. I mean, why would anyone go to a supermarket
> b. Really, why wouldn't they?   anymore?
> c. Who wants to spend all that money?   e. Who wants all those additives in their food?

Will So, Eunha, you were saying you get your groceries delivered now?

Eunha Yeah. Well, some stuff, __like__ bread and milk. I just go online, place my order, and it's
delivered the next day. It's great. I used to hate carrying all those heavy bags. And it saves time. ☐

Will So how about fresh stuff? I mean, _____ fruit, _____ . It's nice to choose it. ☐

Eunha Well, if you don't like something, they'll take it back. _____ , I had some tomatoes that
were too soft one time and they just replaced them. No problem. ☐

Will But what about reading labels on stuff? You can't do that online. I mean, _____ yogurt.
Everyone thinks it's healthy. But some kinds are full of sugar and food coloring. ☐
You really have to read the labels on everything!

Eunha Well, I just order my usual things, _____ milk and cheese and stuff. So, . . .

Lesson D [Reading] Know your pests

A **Prepare** In what ways are ants pests? Scan the online article, and underline evidence of ants as pests.

Ants: are they all bad?

1 There are more than 12,000 species of ant around the world. They are generally thought of as pests – just go to any supermarket, and you will find a variety of products designed to help you get rid of them. It is certainly annoying when ants get into the kitchen or show up uninvited to a picnic, and obviously, it is painful to be stung! However, are all ants pests, or can some ants be beneficial?

2 A pest is an insect or a small animal that is a threat to the environment, the economy, or human health. ☐ Of all the pests in the world, fire ants are one of the most annoying – and most dangerous. These tiny red ants, originally from South America, were introduced by accident in the southern U.S. in the 1930s, where a moist and warm climate has enabled the number of ants to increase dramatically in states like Alabama and Florida. Today, fire-ant colonies cover more than 1 million square kilometers in this region and cause more than $6 billion in economic losses every year, including medical expenses and damage to crops.

3 Fire ants are aggressive, and their stings can be dangerous. ☐ Furthermore, the economic damage caused by the ants, which eat small plants before they have grown to full size, is devastating. This has been the painful discovery that people from the Philippines, China, and Australia have made in the last 25 years as fire ants have spread in these countries at an alarming rate, due to trade with the U.S. But why are ants a problem in these countries and not in their native South America?

4 Fire-ant colonies have been prevented from growing too quickly in South America as a result of parasites, viruses, and competition with other ant species. A lack of these natural enemies is believed to be one factor that has allowed fire ants to spread quickly in other parts of the world and is believed to contribute to their survival. ☐ Moreover, this growth is not slowing down: scientists believe that fire ants might well spread across half the planet.

5 So what does this mean? Is it all bad? It is well known that earthworms are a farmer's best friend. They improve the quality of farmland by turning over the soil. This helps to get air into the soil, which enables more water to be absorbed and crop production to increase. However, what many people don't realize is that many species of ant are even more beneficial to soil than earthworms. ☐

6 Some ants also act as natural pesticides, killing harmful crop-eating insects and protecting plants. In fact, the earliest known use of biological pest management – by Chinese orange growers – was described in a book written by Chinese botanist Hsi Han in AD 340. Bamboo "bridges" were provided by the farmers, which allowed the ants to move from tree to tree in order to reach and kill the "bad" insects.

7 Ants are also important distributors of seeds and play an important role in pollination. ☐ In desert areas, for example, some plants depend on ants alone to harvest and "plant" their seeds. Ants have become even more important since it was discovered that crops are being threatened by a mysterious decline in the bee population in recent years. As more bees die and their colonies collapse, ants could prevent the disappearance of bees from becoming a devastating crisis.

8 We may continue to think of ants as pests, but they perform a number of helpful jobs. It might be difficult, but try to remember this the next time you get stung by a fire ant, or an army of ants invades your kitchen.

B **Read for main ideas** Where do these sentences fit in the article? Write the letters a–f in the boxes in the article. There is one extra sentence.

a. For example, only 85 years after their introduction, there were five times more fire ants per kilometer in the U.S. than in their native South America.
b. In some cases, they can be just as effective as bees and flies in pollinating crops.
c. Queen ants can fly up to one-quarter of a mile on their own.
d. Take fire ants, for example.
e. Medical attention is sometimes required after people are stung, and small animals can even die from multiple fire-ant stings.
f. It has been discovered, for example, that the holes most ants make in the earth allow more rain to be absorbed.

C **Check your understanding** Read the article again. Then answer the questions.

1. How many species of ant have been discovered in the world?

_____

2. How much does fire-ant damage cost the U.S. economy each year?

_____

3. Why have fire-ant colonies spread to other countries outside of the Americas?

_____

4. How do ants benefit the soil?

_____

5. How do ants act as pesticides?

_____

6. Why are ants considered even more important now?

_____

D **Focus on vocabulary** Complete the definitions with the noun forms of the verbs in the box. Find the words in the article.

| disappear | discover | lose | pollinate | produce | survive | threaten |

1. Something that is a _____ is likely to cause damage or be a danger. (para. 2)
2. If you experience _____ , you fail to keep something that is of value. (para. 2)
3. A _____ is something that had not been known before. (para. 3)
4. The _____ of something is its ability to stay alive. (para. 4)
5. The process of growing plants for food is known as crop _____ . (para. 5)
6. _____ requires the deposit of pollen for fertilization. (para. 7)
7. The _____ of something happens when it stops existing. (para. 7)

About you

E **React** Were there any facts in the article that surprised or troubled you? Explain.

_____

_____

_____

_____

Writing A report for a science class

A Look at the graphs and charts, and complete the sentences.

1. Number of people stung by fire ants

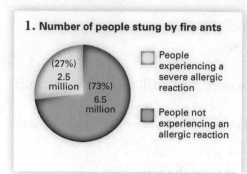

(27%)
2.5 million   (73%)
6.5 million

☐ People experiencing a severe allergic reaction

☐ People not experiencing an allergic reaction

2.

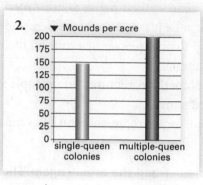

▼ Mounds per acre

single-queen colonies   multiple-queen colonies

3. Economic losses

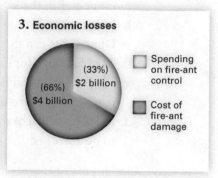

(33%)
$2 billion

(66%)
$4 billion

☐ Spending on fire-ant control

☐ Cost of fire-ant damage

1. Approximately 2.5 million people per year experience a severe allergic reaction to fire-ant stings, which accounts for _____ percent of all victims.

2. In areas with fire-ant colonies with just one queen, there are nearly _____ mounds per acre. This rises to _____ per acre in areas that have colonies with more than one queen.

3. Fire-ant control accounts for _____ percent of the economic losses that fire ants are responsible for.

B Circle the correct preposition. Then complete the report with the expressions in the box.

+/– about / approximately / roughly	– under / less than
+ over / more than	>| nearly / almost / up to

The dramatic rise **on / in** the number of fire-ant colonies in the U.S. is a cause for concern. In areas with large fire-ant colonies, _____ (>\|) 60 percent of the population is stung every year, which means that _____ (+/–) 9 million people are stung by fire ants each year. Of those 9 million, _____ (+/–) 27 percent experience a severe allergic reaction and some even die.

Currently, Americans spend _____ (+) $2 billion on fire-ant control and fire-ant damage accounts for _____ (>\|) $4 billion each year. What is worrisome is that there has been a rise **in / by** colonies that have more than one queen. Areas with single-queen colonies can have _____ (>\|) 150 mounds per acre. However, in areas with multiple-queen colonies, the number of mounds has been known to increase **in / by** _____ (+/–) 33 percent. While the use of chemical pesticides has caused a decline **of / in** fire-ant activity **of / by** _____ (>\|) 90 percent, it has been found that the ants come back in less than one month if the pesticides are not reapplied. Some success has been reported by farmers controlling fire ants with other insects.

C Editing Correct the sentences. There is one error in each sentence.

1. The number of countries that are affected by the spread of fire ants has grown up.

2. The rise of the number of multiple-queen colonies is a cause for concern.

3. Where multiple-queen colonies are found, the number of mounds rises up significantly.

4. Chemical pesticides can cause the number of fire-ant mounds to fall down dramatically.

5. Farmers who have used other insects to control fire ants have experienced a decline of ant colonies.

D Write a report for a science class with the title *The rise in fire-ant colonies – a cause for concern?* Use the model in Exercise B to help you. Then check your report for errors.

Listening extra Smart foods

A Make a list of five foods that you think are good for you.

_____ _____ _____ _____ _____

B ⬇ Listen to a radio interview with an expert on food nutrition. Check (✔) the effects of foods that are mentioned in the interview. There are two extra effects.

about foods that. . .

☐ a. can improve your mood
☐ b. can prevent you from getting cancer
☐ c. can help lower your blood pressure
☐ d. can protect you against heart disease
☐ e. can prevent your skin from aging
☐ f. may protect your brain cells from deteriorating
☐ g. helps you to build strong muscles
☐ h. may make headaches go away
☐ i. may reduce the risk of depression

C ⬇ Listen again. Match each smart food with its health benefits in Exercise B. Write the letters a–i. Some benefits go with more than one food.

1. blueberries _____

2. avocados _____

3. coffee _____

4. fish _____

D ⬇ Listen again. Circle the best option to complete the sentences.

1. The guest on the show _____ .
   a. has published books on healthy foods   b. is a specialist doctor
   c. specializes in mood therapy
2. The host suggests eating avocados _____ .
   a. in salads   b. on sandwiches   c. every day
3. Coffee has particular health benefits for _____ .
   a. old people   b. young people   c. middle-aged people
4. Fish should be eaten _____ .
   a. every day   b. once or twice a week   c. once a month
5. The best fish to eat is _____ salmon.
   a. farmed   b. wild   c. canned

About you

E Answer the questions with your own ideas and opinions.

1. Which information in the interview was new or surprising to you?

_____

_____

2. Does the interview make you want to eat more of any of the foods mentioned? Which ones?

_____

_____

Now complete the _Unit 8 Progress chart_ on page 98.   Unit 8: Food science   **65**

Unit 9 Success and happiness

Lesson A **Vocabulary** Expressions with *get*

A Circle the best option to complete the *get* expressions in the article.

Successful entrepreneurs Caterina Fake and Stewart Butterfield got **anywhere / to the top** by making their careers on the Internet. As co-founders of one of the first photo-sharing sites, Flickr, they helped change the way people use the Internet. So how did they both get **to be / under way** two of the world's most successful Internet entrepreneurs?

Caterina Fake   Stewart Butterfield

Caterina describes herself as "always curious," and her ability to learn new things is perhaps the quality that has helped her get **ahead / on with**. Stewart didn't study business or computer science, but he didn't let that get **anywhere / in his way**. With two degrees in philosophy, he simply got **on with / ahead** the job and learned about business along the way.

Not all products get **off to a good start / to be**, but Caterina believes that good products will ultimately sell themselves – especially on the Internet. Users of Flickr, for example, contributed to its development once it got **on with / under way**. Then, after it got **off the ground / in the way**, there was no stopping it.

So, what lessons can new entrepreneurs learn from their story? Perhaps that you won't get **anywhere / you down** by worrying about what you don't know and not to let initial problems get **off to a good start / you down**. If you know you have a great product, stay with it.

B Complete the conversation with a correct form of the *get* expressions in the box.

get ahead	get in (your) way	get off to a good start	get (me) down	get to the top
get anywhere	get off the ground	get on with	get to be	get under way

A Did you hear that I failed my final exam? It's really _____ me _____ . I don't know what to do. I just can't seem to _____ my life right now.

B I know, but you won't _____ if you don't take control and do something positive.

A Yeah. The thing is, though, that I was sick when my classes started. So I didn't _____ . I mean, it wasn't a good way to begin the semester. Then when all the courses _____ , I felt completely lost.

B Well, a lot of successful people never graduated from college. Take Mark Zuckerberg. He dropped out of college, but he _____ one of the richest people in the world. He managed to _____ in life and be successful. In fact, he _____ of his profession.

A I guess so. But I'm not going to _____ a company like Facebook _____ , am I? I mean, I couldn't start up a company like that.

B I guess not. I'm just saying don't let one failure _____ your _____ . Don't let it stop you from being successful.

Lesson A (Grammar) Talking about *all* and *none*

A Circle the correct determiners to complete the conversations.

1. *A* Would you say that **neither / both / all** your family members are successful in some way? I mean, like, your parents and brothers and sisters and everyone.
   B Well, I'd say that **neither / both / all** my parents are successful, because they raised a happy family. **No / None / All** family is successful if it's not happy. At least, not in my opinion.
   A I guess so. Do **none / all of / every** your brothers and sisters say the same?
   B Yeah. We all have happy memories. When we were little, **every / none of / all** kid in the neighborhood used to come to our house and **neither / each / all** kid was made to feel welcome. **None of / Neither / Neither of** my parents ever complained about how many kids were there.

2. *A* What makes a person successful, do you think?
   B Good question. If you think about **each / every / all of** the really successful actors and athletes – they work really hard to get to the top of their careers. You know, **none of / neither / no** these people just let things happen. They put in really long hours, and **all / neither / every** their hard work pays off in the end.

3. *A* How did you decide on your major? I mean, did you ask your family for advice?
   B Well, no, not really. **None of / No / Neither** my relatives went to college. So I talked to my teachers and advisors about different careers, but honestly, **no / every / none of** the information they gave me was really that useful. I think you have to choose for yourself. I mean, **none / no / each** advice is really that useful. So yeah, I looked at law and accounting and took some classes, but I decided that **all / neither / both** profession was for me.

B Rewrite the sentences by replacing the underlined words with the determiners in parentheses. Make any necessary changes to the sentences.

1. <u>Every</u> business student dreams of setting up a successful company. (All)
   All business students dream of setting up a successful company.

2. <u>All</u> the students in my class last year wanted to start a business. (Each)
   _____

3. My <u>two</u> best friends got new companies under way last year. (Both)
   _____

4. <u>Their</u> companies didn't get off to a good start. (Neither)
   _____

5. My <u>two</u> friends can't say they've made any money yet. (Neither of)
   _____

6. <u>All</u> their enthusiasm hasn't been lost, though. (None of)
   _____

7. After all, <u>it's not possible that a</u> business can be an immediate success. (No)
   _____

About you

C Answer *A*'s questions in Exercise A with information that is true for you.

1. _____
2. _____
3. _____

Lesson B   Grammar   Adding information

A Is the *-ing* form in each sentence a reduced relative clause (RC), an event that happens at the same time (ST), or the subject (S) or object (O) of a verb? Write RC, ST, S, or O.

1. I enjoyed my time in high school, studying lots of different subjects. _____
2. I'll never forget walking out of my last high school class. _____
3. I left that class with tears in my eyes, feeling sad that it was all over. _____
4. I have so many friends trying to find jobs with high salaries. _____
5. But my philosophy is that making a lot of money isn't everything. _____
6. Some of the people I know working in banks are miserable. _____

B Use an *-ing* form to rewrite the underlined part of each sentence in these anecdotes.

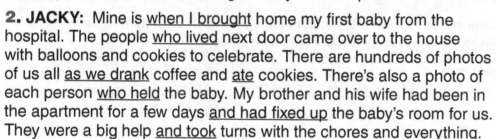

My happiest moment in life so far . . .

1. MICHAEL: Probably my happiest moment was <u>when I got</u> my grades for my last year of college. I remember <u>that I watched</u> the mail carrier as he walked toward our mailbox. I ran outside and got the mail from him, and stood there with the envelope in my hand <u>and didn't dare</u> to open it. Eventually, I did open it <u>and I was trembling</u>. I read the page twice <u>and didn't believe</u> my eyes: straight A's. I was so happy because I knew that there would be so many opportunities <u>that were opening up</u> for me. And also <u>the fact that I got</u> straight A's showed my parents that I'd really made the most of college – they were so proud.

2. JACKY: Mine is <u>when I brought</u> home my first baby from the hospital. The people <u>who lived</u> next door came over to the house with balloons and cookies to celebrate. There are hundreds of photos of us all <u>as we drank</u> coffee and <u>ate</u> cookies. There's also a photo of each person <u>who held</u> the baby. My brother and his wife had been in the apartment for a few days <u>and had fixed up</u> the baby's room for us. They were a big help <u>and took</u> turns with the chores and everything.

3. LEE: My happiest moment is <u>the time I went</u> on vacation when I was eight. My parents looked so happy <u>as they walked</u> along the beach <u>and held</u> hands. My sister and I ran ahead, <u>and tried</u> to be the first one to get to the man <u>who sold</u> ice cream. My sister let me win, <u>and pretended</u> to get tired before we reached the truck. Then we sat on the sand <u>and ate</u> these big ice creams with chocolate sprinkles <u>and looked for</u> "white horses" in the ocean waves. Magical.

1. Probably my happiest moment was getting my grades . . .

About you

C Write an anecdote about a happy moment in your life. Use *-ing* forms.

_____

_____

_____

_____

Lesson C Conversation strategies

A Complete *B*'s answers using the words in parentheses and any expression in the box.
(Use *in terms of* only once.) Then write your own answers to the questions.

as far as . . . goes / go	as far as . . . is / are concerned	in terms of	when it comes to

1. *A* What is happiness?
   B I think you can define happiness _____ . (having no worries)

2. *A* What makes you happy?
   B _____ , happiness is just being home with my family. (my everyday life)

3. *A* Why do people think money will make them happy?
   B I don't know. _____ , you don't need money. (being happy)

4. *A* Do you think you can teach yourself how to be happy?
   B I guess so. Though _____ , it's not easy for some people. (learning how to be happy)

About you

B Match the questions and answers. Write the letters a–e in the boxes. Then write your own
answers using the expressions *as far as I'm concerned, as far as I can tell*, and *as far as I know*.

1. Are you generally a positive person? ☐ _____
2. Are your friends happy? ☐ _____
3. Do you think working in a great job makes people happy? ☐ _____
4. Have you ever been really unhappy? ☐ _____
5. What kinds of things make people most unhappy, do you think? ☐ _____

a. As far as I can tell, it's relationship issues, mostly, like breakups.
b. Not really. As far as I'm concerned, life's too short. You just have to be positive about things.
c. I guess. Well, as far as I know, people say that I'm a fun guy to be around.
d. It depends. As far as I'm concerned, that's not a big deal for me, but for my friends, it is.
e. As far as I can tell, they are.

C Circle the correct options. Then complete each conversation with a correct expression in the box.

as far as I can tell	as far as I know	as far as I'm concerned

1. *A* Do you think Jerry and his fiancée will be happy? They haven't known each other long.
   B I don't know. When it comes to **divorce / settling down**, it's hard to know. I mean, he hasn't
   even met her family yet.
   A Actually, _____ , she doesn't have any close family.

2. *A* We had the best time last year, exploring the island. Everyone's so happy there.
   B Well, it is beautiful, and as far as **lifestyle / work** goes, it's perfect. No stress. Nice weather.
   A Yeah, _____ , I could happily move there tomorrow!

3. *A* So, how are things going? You seem to have a lot going on.
   B Yeah, as far as my **job / home life** is concerned, I'm not really enjoying it. You know, just in
   terms of the **type / amount** of work. I mean, I'm at my desk, working till ten every night.
   And _____ , my boss doesn't appreciate it.

Lesson D Reading What is happiness?

A Prepare Which of the following factors do you think are most important in determining a person's happiness? Check (✔) six factors.

☐ age   ☐ education   ☐ family   ☐ income   ☐ looks   ☐ religious beliefs
☐ attitude   ☐ expectations   ☐ friends   ☐ job satisfaction   ☐ marriage   ☐ wealth

B Read for main ideas Read the article. Which factors in Exercise A are most important, according to the article? Which are less important?

What makes people HAPPY?

1   Do you know what makes you happy? People often think money is the key to happiness. While it is true that wealthy populations are happier than poor ones, seeking wealth is rarely the answer for individuals, according to many experts. In fact, once the basic needs, such as home, food, clothing, etc., are met, people in wealthier nations are only slightly happier when their incomes improve. Even lottery winners do not experience greater happiness after the thrill of winning has faded.

2   If not wealth, then what does make us happy? Most experts agree there are multiple factors contributing to happiness. Surprisingly, the research suggests that income, age, good looks, and education are only weakly linked to happiness, whereas internal factors, such as personality and attitude, hold the strongest links. Expectation plays a huge role, too. Take Denmark, for instance; although it is ranked the happiest nation in the world, its inhabitants report low expectations, according to some studies. On the other hand, people in the U.S. have higher expectations but lower levels of happiness than the Danes.

3   The evidence also suggests that happiness is, to some extent, relative. For example, in one study, college students were asked to choose between a world in which they earned $50,000 a year but everyone else earned $25,000 on average, and a world in which they earned $100,000 a year, while others earned an average of $250,000. The majority voted for the first world, because they were willing to have less, provided they were in a better position compared to others.

4   Perhaps some people are born happier than others. Studies indicate that identical twins have similar levels of happiness, and even twins separated at birth turn out equally happy. Some researchers claim there is a "set level" of happiness we are born with and that we automatically come back to. On the other hand, experts agree that people can do a lot to control their own well-being, despite their inborn characteristics.

5   Not surprisingly, friendship, family, and social networks appear to boost levels of happiness. In another study of college students, the happiest 10 percent reported strong ties with friends and family. Furthermore, those students had the lowest levels of depression. Religious faith is also frequently linked with happiness, although researchers are not sure why. Perhaps it is because of participation in strong social networks, common among religious people. Marriage and a sense of purpose at work are directly linked with happiness as well. In fact, two major events leading to depression are the loss of a spouse and the loss of a job, according to researchers. All of these factors can be important contributors to happiness or unhappiness.

6   Should political leaders then support policies meant to increase their citizens' happiness? Certainly the eradication of poverty is an important goal for all governments to pursue. Moreover, wars bring about the greatest misery, so peace may be one of the most important priorities. However, there is controversy about how much governments can actually do to stimulate happiness.

7   When it comes to happiness, many factors are involved, yet the ingredient that stands out most is expectation. People with low expectations are pleasantly surprised when things turn out better than they had thought. This doesn't mean pessimism or lack of goals will lead to happiness, but realistic expectations just might. As the saying goes, "If you expect the worst, you won't be disappointed."

C Read for detail Read the article again. Are the sentences true or false? Write T or F. Then correct the false sentences.

1. Overall, people in wealthy countries are ~~less happy~~ *happier* than people in poor nations. _F_

2. Being good-looking makes you happier than other people. _____

3. People are happier when they think their situation is better than other people's. _____

4. You can't do anything to change the level of happiness you were born with. _____

5. Religious people may have high levels of happiness because they have good jobs. _____

6. Researchers say losing a job or losing your home can lead to serious depression. _____

7. People with low expectations are often the happiest. _____

D Focus on vocabulary Find each underlined word in the article, and circle the correct synonym. Then answer the questions with your own information.

1. What makes the population of a country happy? (para. 1)
   a. government   b. workers   c. people

2. Do you know any people who seek wealth rather than happiness? (para. 1)
   a. try to find   b. can't find   c. reject

3. How can people make themselves wealthier? (para. 1)
   a. richer   b. happier   c. more satisfied

4. Do you think your nation is generally happy? Why or why not? (para. 2)
   a. country   b. city   c. continent

5. What problems might there be if there were too many inhabitants in a country? (para. 2)
   a. rules   b. houses   c. people

6. What other things should governments analyze – apart from economic trends? (para. 5)
   a. study   b. reject   c. accept

7. Should employers have policies for keeping workers happy? (para. 6)
   a. benefits   b. plans   c. culture

8. Are most of your country's citizens well-educated? (para. 6)
   a. people   b. politicians   c. teenagers

9. What are the priorities in your life? Wealth? Family? Happiness? (para. 6)
   a. important things   b. best things   c. unimportant things

10. How can the government stimulate the economy to grow? (para. 6)
    a. allow   b. encourage   c. expect

About you **E React** Answer the questions with information that is true for you.

1. Which facts in the article surprised you? Which ones didn't?

   _____

2. Think of someone you know who always seems happy. Why do you think that is?

   _____

3. What do you think you can do to be happier?

   _____

Writing A paragraph in an essay

A Circle the correct options to complete the paragraph from an essay.

Why should people be more involved in their community?

There are a number of reasons why people should become more involved in community activities. Research shows there are benefits for the community **in addition / as well as** individuals. In terms of the individual, some social psychologists claim that getting involved in your community improves your satisfaction with life **in addition to / furthermore** boosting your levels of happiness. **Moreover, / As well as** the movement Action for Happiness lists connecting with people **and / moreover** doing things for your community as two of the keys to personal happiness. For these reasons alone, community involvement is positive for all residents. Community activities help to build social cohesion, contributing to a sense of well-being. **Furthermore, / In addition to** by taking a positive approach to problems such as graffiti or vandalism, people can also improve their physical environment. In conclusion, each person in a community should be involved in its activities.

B Rewrite the sentences, replacing the words in bold with the expressions given in parentheses. Make any necessary changes to the word order, grammar, or punctuation.

1. It is important to tell people about the good things going on in a community **and** its problems. (as well as) _____

2. A community newsletter can advertise local events **and** inform people about local news. (in addition to) _____

3. A website might **also** encourage the younger members of the community to be more involved. (Moreover) _____

4. As far as litter is concerned, having cleanup days can be fun **and also** effective. (as well as)

   _____

5. **Also**, people are less likely to litter in places that are already clean. (Furthermore)

   _____

6. Holding special events can create a stronger community **and** make the neighborhood a nicer place to live. (in addition to) _____

C Editing Correct the mistakes in these sentences. One sentence is correct.

1. Neighborhood activities benefit the community as well as makes the volunteers happy.

2. As well as provide practical help, community activities contribute to social cohesion.

3. Moreover, some communities organize events for families as well as older people to create a sense of belonging.

4. In addition to encourage volunteering, some high schools offer credits for community work.

5. Picking up trash gives volunteers a sense of satisfaction in addition discouraging them from littering the streets.

6. In addition to, cleanup days create a more pleasant environment.

D Write a paragraph to answer the essay question in Exercise A. Use at least two of the expressions in Exercise A to add ideas to your paragraph. Then check your paragraph for errors.

Listening extra Does happiness lead to success?

A Match the two parts of each sentence. Write the letters a–d. Then check (✔) the sentences you agree with.

☐ 1. Happiness leads to ____
☐ 2. Providing good education and health programs results in ____
☐ 3. It is true that ____
☐ 4. Being successful helps you avoid ____

a. being happy makes you healthier.
b. success.
c. poor health.
d. happier citizens.

B ⬇ Listen to two students talk about a lecture. Check (✔) the correct answers to the questions.

1. What do the two students talk about?
   ☐ a. The content of a lecture they attended
   ☐ b. The length of the lecture

2. What kind of conversation do they have?
   ☐ a. It's a friendly discussion, sharing different ideas.
   ☐ b. It's an argument, and they're trying to make each other see a different point of view.

3. What topic do they move on to at the end of their conversation?
   ☐ a. Their professor's health issues
   ☐ b. Programs that can help make the citizens of a country happy

C ⬇ Listen again. Circle the correct option to complete each sentence.

1. Rob's grandparents were successful as far as their **work / family life** was concerned.
2. Laurie suggests that, as far as she is concerned, work is less important than having **a nice lifestyle / close relationships**.
3. Rob read research from a university that said **happy / educated** people become successful.
4. The research also suggested that positive people don't **work / get sick** as much.
5. Laurie thinks the research **makes sense / doesn't make sense**.
6. In his lecture, Professor Blake **talked / didn't talk** about the things a country can do to make its citizens happy.

About you

D ⬇ Listen again to the conversation. How would you respond? Complete the sentences with your own ideas.

1. Well, as far as I'm concerned, _____

_____

_____

2. As far as I can tell, _____

_____

_____

3. Well, when it comes to _____

_____

_____

Now complete the *Unit 9 Progress chart* on page 100.

Going places

Lesson A Vocabulary Describing travel experiences

A **Circle the correct adjectives to complete the conversation.**

A Your trip to the Amazon sounds really **fascinated** / ⟨**fascinating**⟩.

B It was! The wildlife was just **amazed** / **amazing** – we saw monkeys, and pink dolphins, and snakes.

A Weren't you, well, **frightened** / **frightening** at all? I mean, I read that the Amazon has some **frightened** / **frightening** animals, like those huge snakes. What do you call them?

B Anacondas. Yeah, to be honest, I was **terrified** / **terrifying** when the guide told us about them. I guess I felt a little more **encouraged** / **encouraging** when he said nothing had ever happened on his tours. The worst thing we heard about was the piranhas, though.

A Yeah? Why's that?

B Well, he said they can kill you in minutes – that was the most **surprised** / **surprising** thing for me.

A Really? It all sounds totally **terrified** / **terrifying**. But anyway, were you canoeing?

B Well, we canoed a couple of days. Though I have to say with the heat and humidity, it was pretty **challenged** / **challenging**.

A I bet. I'm just really **impressed** / **impressive** you went canoeing at all. It must have been **exhausted** / **exhausting**.

B Yeah. Kind of. With the change in climate, it was pretty **tired** / **tiring**. But it was fun.

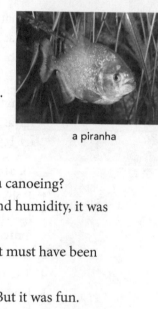
an anaconda

a piranha

B **Complete the blog post with a correct adjective form of the verbs given.**

BLOG   HOTELS   RENTALS   TOURS

My friend and I decided we wanted to go on a _challenging_ (challenge) adventure this year, and to make a long story short, we ended up in Ecuador! After arriving in the capital city, Quito, we took a small plane into the rain forest. It was only a 16-seater, and since I'd never traveled in such a small plane before, I was far from _____ (relax). In fact, I was _____ (terrify)! The landing was bumpy, but after such a long and _____ (tire) day, I was just happy to be on solid ground.
We had a light dinner at the camp, and crawled into our sleeping bags just after it got dark. However, in spite of being _____ (exhaust), I didn't sleep very well. I guess I was overtired. The next day, we got up early and started our river trip in a canoe. It was the rainy season, so I thought it was _____ (surprise) to see so many animals and birds. I told the guide I was a bit _____ (puzzle) because I hadn't expected to see so much wildlife. He explained that the animals in the forest are very active during rainy season because more food is available to them. We learned so many _____ (fascinate) things and had such a great time. I think I'm going to be feeling a bit _____ (depress) going back to work.

Lesson A Grammar Reporting what people say

A Two friends went on a hike last month. Complete the sentences with reported speech. Add *him* or *them* where necessary.

1. "We want to go hiking in the national park."

   Mike said <u>they wanted to go hiking in the national park</u> .

2. "There may be a storm later today. You should be prepared."

   The park ranger informed _____ . He also said _____ .

3. "I have a map, and we won't go too far."

   Mike said _____ and that _____ .

4. "We're just going for a short hike. We plan to do a longer hike tomorrow."

   Luci explained _____ . She also told _____ .

5. "You must stay on the trails or you could get lost."

   The park ranger told _____ .

6. "Some areas are dangerous because they've gotten very wet recently."

   The park ranger also explained _____ .

7. "We know the park well." "We used to hike here a lot in college."

   Luci and Mike said _____ . Mike said _____ .

8. "You can always take shelter in the huts along the trails."

   The park ranger told _____ .

B Complete the anecdote with a correct form of the verbs given. Add an indirect object pronoun (*me, him*) or no indirect object pronoun (-) after the reporting verbs *said, told,* and *explained.*

When I decided to go to Bogotá, Colombia, my friend Joaquín gave me plenty of tips about where to go, what to see, etc. Joaquín told ___me___ that I ___had to___ (have to) visit the cathedral. He said ___–___ no one _____ (should) leave the city without seeing it. He also told _____ about the Iglesia de San Francisco. He explained _____ that it _____ (be) the city's oldest church and that I _____ (will) find it amazing. Joaquín knows I love museums, so he said _____ he _____ (can) recommend a few for me to see. He said _____ that he _____ (think) that I _____ (might) like the Gold Museum and the Archaeological Museum. I told _____ that one place I _____ (look forward to) visiting _____ (be) the Botero Donation. Joaquín explained _____ that Botero, a well-known Colombian artist, _____ (donate) over 100 pieces of art to his country in the year 2000 and that they _____ (can) be found on exhibit in Bogotá. I told _____ that I _____ (must) see that.

About you

C Think of a conversation you had recently with someone before you went on a trip or simply went shopping. Report three things you said or the other person said to you. Use *said, told,* and *explained.*

My roommate and I went shopping last weekend. He said it would rain and that . . .

1. _____

2. _____

3. _____

Lesson B Grammar Reporting questions/instructions

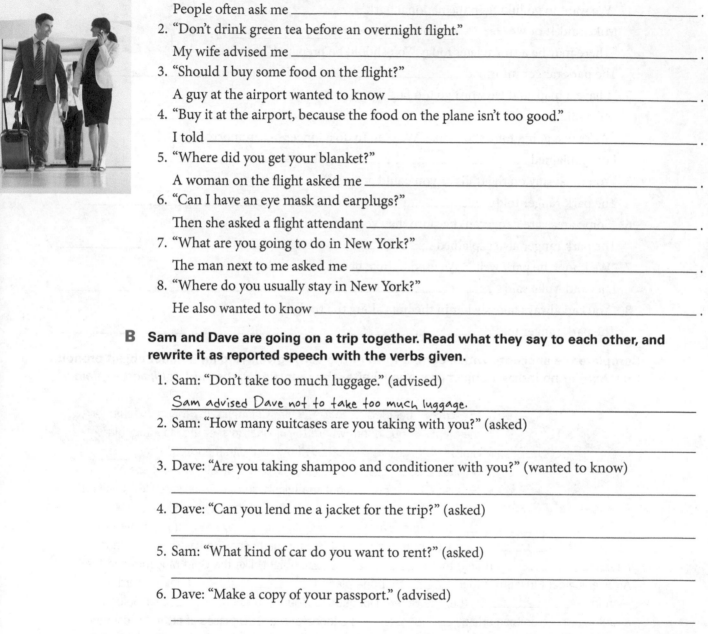

A Paulo has just arrived in New York and is telling a co-worker about his flight. Complete
the sentences with the reported speech. Sometimes more than one answer is possible.

1. "Do you always travel with just one bag?"

   People often ask me _____ .

2. "Don't drink green tea before an overnight flight."

   My wife advised me _____ .

3. "Should I buy some food on the flight?"

   A guy at the airport wanted to know _____ .

4. "Buy it at the airport, because the food on the plane isn't too good."

   I told _____ .

5. "Where did you get your blanket?"

   A woman on the flight asked me _____ .

6. "Can I have an eye mask and earplugs?"

   Then she asked a flight attendant _____ .

7. "What are you going to do in New York?"

   The man next to me asked me _____ .

8. "Where do you usually stay in New York?"

   He also wanted to know _____ .

B Sam and Dave are going on a trip together. Read what they say to each other, and
rewrite it as reported speech with the verbs given.

1. Sam: "Don't take too much luggage." (advised)

   Sam advised Dave not to take too much luggage.

2. Sam: "How many suitcases are you taking with you?" (asked)

   _____

3. Dave: "Are you taking shampoo and conditioner with you?" (wanted to know)

   _____

4. Dave: "Can you lend me a jacket for the trip?" (asked)

   _____

5. Sam: "What kind of car do you want to rent?" (asked)

   _____

6. Dave: "Make a copy of your passport." (advised)

   _____

About you

C Complete four things you could ask a frequent traveler (1–4). Then complete two pieces
of advice to travelers in your country (5–6).

1. I'd like to know if _____ .

2. Can you tell me how _____ ?

3. Can I ask you where _____ ?

4. I've always wanted to know what _____ .

5. I'd advise all travelers to this country _____ .

6. I'd also advise them not _____ .

Lesson C Conversation strategies

A Circle the correct option to complete the conversations.

1. A You know, white-water rafting is not really my thing. Those rafts turn over all the time.
   B **So you mean it's perfectly safe? / So you're saying that it's too dangerous?**

2. A Have you ever gone skydiving?
   B Skydiving? No way! I mean, what if your parachute didn't open?
   A **So I guess you don't want to go on Saturday, then? / So you're saying it's fun?**

3. A You know, I've never wanted to try ski jumping. Imagine flying through the air at that height.
   B **So what you're saying is you're scared of heights? / So you mean you'd try it?**

4. A Come on. Let's go on the roller coaster. There are only a couple of people in line.
   B No. It doesn't look very exciting.
   A **So I guess it's not scary enough for you. / So you're saying you'll try anything?**

B Complete the conversations with . . . *in what way?*

1. A I think bungee jumping is really dangerous.
   B _____ I mean, they check the ropes after every jump.
   A Yeah, but I think I'd rather keep my feet on the ground.

2. A I would love to go into space. It would be so cool!
   B _____ Don't you think it would be kind of scary?
   A Not really. I just think it would be exciting.

3. A Traveling can be life-changing.
   B _____
   A Well, getting to know a different culture and stuff. It changes you.

C Complete the conversation with the appropriate follow-up questions in the box.

a. Challenging in what way?
b. So I guess you won't be interested in doing something with me this weekend, then?
c. So you're saying that a world trip isn't exciting enough for you?
d. So you're saying you'll come?
e. You mean, like take a trip around the world or something?

Alex   Wouldn't you just love to go on the trip of a lifetime someday?

Sofia _____

Alex   No. I was actually thinking about something more challenging.

Sofia _____

Alex   Well, I meant something really exciting – like a trip into space.

Sofia _____

Alex   Right. I just think that seeing the world from space would be amazing – the silence, being
         weightless, and all that. I mean, I just want to do something really different and exciting.

Sofia _____ I was thinking of going mountain biking.

Alex   Actually, that would be fun! Why not?

Sofia _____

Alex   Sure. I'd love to.

Lesson D Reading Independent travel

A **Prepare** What are the advantages and disadvantages of guidebooks for travelers? Write as many ideas as you can think of.

B **Read for main ideas** Find two advantages and two disadvantages of guidebooks that the writer gives. Which of your ideas were mentioned?

Travel guides: blessing or curse?

1 If you've ever planned a trip overseas, you will probably have turned to a guidebook series in your search for information about your chosen destination. There are now dozens of guides available, but this wasn't always the case. The publication of modern guidebooks for travelers on a budget started in the 1970s as independent travel became more popular, especially among young people. There was a clear need for guides that helped independent travelers find their way in unfamiliar or exotic places and that gave honest reviews about places to stay and things to see. One or two enterprising companies answered that need. Then, over the next 30 years, guidebook publishing became a huge business and the range of countries that the books covered expanded quickly. Tony Wheeler, co-founder of one guidebook series, said that ". . . the travel book explosion was led by travelers who got into publishing rather than publishers getting into travel." In other words, the information in these types of travel guides is written by travelers for other travelers and gives insights into destinations that guidebooks had not previously provided.

2 Despite their many advantages to the independent traveler, travel guides may well have a downside, however. It's true that they encourage people to explore new places and be more adventurous; travelers, after all, don't think of themselves as tourists. However, their "insider" tips have long since become mass knowledge, available to everyone. Nowadays, no matter where you are in the world and no matter how remote the destination, you are unlikely to be alone. The chances are that when you look around, you'll see other travelers with a travel guide in their hands. A handful of independent travelers can soon turn into mass tourism as the word about a place gets around.

3 Indeed, one of the biggest threats to once quiet and remote areas – destinations that were not previously on the usual tourist trail – is an ever-increasing number of visitors. Additional tourists can adversely affect once beautiful and peaceful places. They often generate huge amounts of waste, consume resources like water and energy, and may cause problems with already struggling local infrastructures. Furthermore, the development of tourist facilities to cope with a flood of tourists can irreversibly change the traditional culture of a destination.

4 A further effect of travel guides is that people working in the industries related to tourism rely heavily on positive reviews to bring them customers. It may well be that this is good for tourists because it forces up general standards, but what are the effects on businesses that are not mentioned (perhaps because the reviewer didn't go there, or because they were set up after the guide was published, etc.)? A restaurant, store, or hotel could be excellent, but it might not get enough foreign visitors simply because it's not mentioned in the popular guides. If it's not in the guidebook, it doesn't really exist.

5 In spite of these problems, one could argue that the main value of guidebooks is that they create a better awareness among travelers of the country they are visiting. These books go further than offering tips on places to stay, eat, visit, and shop; they include information about the culture, history, and politics of an area, helping their readers to be more knowledgeable about their host country, even though this knowledge can be limited and superficial. In addition, the arrival of independent travelers (the main market for these guidebooks) can sometimes bring badly needed revenue to communities as it develops a tourist industry that employs local people to work in hotels and restaurants and at tourist sites.

6 Nevertheless, while some argue that this kind of tourism can benefit communities, the challenge for all is to manage its negative effects. The responsibility will inevitably rest on host countries, through preserving the local culture and protecting the environment. However, there is a responsibility on travelers too and guidebooks can and should make a contribution to this effort by making their readers sensitive to the issues that travel raises.

C **Check your understanding** Choose the correct option to complete the sentences.

1. Before the 1970s, the writer claims there were _____ guidebooks than there are now.
   a. fewer   b. more   c. better   d. clearer

2. The guidebooks that were published in the 1970s became popular because they were written by people who knew about _____ .
   a. publishing   b. business   c. destinations   d. writing

3. The writer believes that more recent guidebooks encourage independent travelers to go to places that _____ .
   a. have no tourists   b. are full of tourists   c. used to have no tourists   d. want more tourism

4. One problem with tourism that the writer does not mention is _____ .
   a. greater energy use   b. garbage or trash   c. air pollution   d. impact on local services

5. Some people think that guidebooks have a/an _____ value for travelers.
   a. educational   b. economic   c. organizational   d. political

6. The writer concludes that it is the responsibility of _____ to reduce the negative effects of tourism.
   a. guidebooks   b. travelers   c. everyone   d. host communities

7. Overall, the writer has a/an _____ view of guidebooks and tourism.
   a. negative   b. positive   c. balanced   d. optimistic

D **Understanding inference** Check (✔) the statements that the writer suggests are true.

☐ 1. Guidebooks that were published in the 1970s were only for young people.

☐ 2. These guidebooks included information that no one had published before.

☐ 3. Independent travelers are not typical tourists.

☐ 4. Guidebooks can contribute to making quiet places into tourist destinations.

☐ 5. Real travelers will look for restaurants that are not in guidebooks.

☐ 6. A guidebook really helps you get to know a country well.

E **Focus on vocabulary** Find the words in the article that are synonyms for the words in bold. Rewrite the sentences, using the synonyms.

1. An increase in the number of tourists can **have a negative impact on** an area. (para. 3)
   An increase in the number of tourists can adversely affect an area.

2. Tourists often **produce a lot of trash** in the areas they visit. (para. 3)
   _____

3. The arrival of more tourists often means the **building** of more tourist facilities. (para. 3)
   _____

4. Reviews are beneficial to tourists because they raise standards in **businesses** that are connected with tourism. (para. 4)
   _____

5. Hotel and restaurant owners in tourist areas **are extremely dependent** on good reviews to attract foreign visitors. (para. 4)
   _____

6. Guidebooks help tourists to develop a better **understanding** of the country they are visiting. (para. 5)
   _____

7. The **income** that tourists bring can be helpful to local communities. (para. 5)
   _____

8. The tourist industry **hires** people from the local area to work in tourist facilities. (para. 5)
   _____

Writing A survey article

Reviews of cities, restaurants, hotels, and attractions are readily available on travel websites. However, are reviews useful and would you use them before planning a trip? Why or why not?

A Ask your friends and family the survey question above, and take notes on their views.

B Read the two extracts from a survey article in a student magazine. Circle the expressions in the extracts that contrast ideas.

Are reviews useful?

• *Reviews are useless!*

Reviews on travel websites are increasingly popular, but I wanted to find out whether travelers thought they were useful. My survey shows that most people tend to read travel websites. (However,) they have mixed feelings about them. Although reviews can be fun or interesting, many people said that the information in them is not always up to date. In fact, most people said they ignore reviews despite the useful information that they might contain. A receptionist in a hotel said . . .

• *Reviews are useful!*

Online reviews are said to make traveling easier. I asked some tourists whether they thought reviews were worth reading. Interestingly enough, even though many travelers think that reviews are not always accurate, most say that the advantages outweigh the disadvantages. It is true that any review is only the personal opinion of one person. Nevertheless, most people think that without reviews, it would be more difficult to plan a vacation. We need reviews in spite of their limitations.

C Editing Correct the mistakes in these sentences from survey articles. Change the expression in bold, or the punctuation, or both. Sometimes more than one answer is possible.

1. **In spite of** reviews are opinions, they are a useful source of information.
   Although/Even though reviews are opinions, they are a useful source of information.

2. **Despite** reviews make restaurants busier, they ensure that general standards improve.
   _____

3. Reviews are a good thing **although** the problems that they may cause.
   _____

4. Reviews might not always be up to date. **Even though** travelers generally like to read them.
   _____

5. **Although** the disadvantages of tourism in remote areas, there are benefits such as employment.
   _____

6. Most people still enjoy their vacations **although** the crowds of tourists in some resorts.
   _____

D Write an article to answer the survey question. Give examples of the things your friends or family said. Then check your article for errors.

Listening extra An eco-tour

A Eco-tourism is traveling in a responsible way, which doesn't harm the environment. What words and expressions would you expect to hear in a conversation about an eco-tour? Write four more ideas.

amazing   rain forest   relaxing   wildlife

_____ _____ _____ _____

B 🔽 **Listen to the conversation. Check (✔) the best sentence to complete the summary of the speaker's views.**

Rick believes that the countries he visited . . .

☐ a. don't do anything to protect the local environment.

☐ b. benefit greatly from eco-tourism.

☐ c. should develop their eco-tourism industries.

C 🔽 **Listen again. Are the sentences true or false? Write T or F. Correct the false sentences.**

1. Rick said that he was tired of beach vacations. _____
2. He told Haley that he enjoyed the eco-tour, but the places they stayed weren't very impressive. _____
3. Haley asked whether eco-tourism had a negative impact on the environment. _____
4. Rick explained that monkeys were still afraid of the tourists. _____
5. Rick said they had used local transportation and restaurants. _____
6. Rick thinks eco-tourism is a positive thing overall. _____

D 🔽 **Listen again and complete the sentences with the missing numbers.**

1. Rick said one of the places they visited got over _____ tourists each year.
2. Rick's tour guide said that tourist numbers had increased by _____ percent in recent years.
3. The guide also mentioned that one of the national parks had up to _____ visitors each day.
4. Rick said he had paid a $_____ entrance fee at one of the nature reserves.
5. The country that Rick visited earns over $_____ in revenue from producing coffee.

About you

E 🔽 **Listen again to the last part of the conversation. What advantages of eco-tourism does Rick mention? Write notes. Do you agree with him? Write your response below.**

1. _____

2. _____

3. _____

Your response:

_____

_____

_____

Now complete the *Unit 10 Progress chart* on page 101.   Unit 10: Going places   **81**

Lesson A Vocabulary Describing wedding customs

A Match the definitions with the words. Write the letters a–h.

1. This person finds someone a partner. _____
2. This man has just gotten married. _____
3. This woman has just gotten married. _____
4. This man helps the groom. _____
5. These women help the bride. _____
6. The mother and father of the man who has just gotten married. _____
7. At a Western-style ceremony, they show guests where to sit. _____
8. The couple that has just gotten married. _____

a. best man
b. bride
c. bridesmaids
d. groom
e. groomsmen
f. matchmaker
g. newlyweds
h. parents of the groom

B Complete the sentences with the words and phrases in the box.

aisle	bachelor	civil ceremony	host	reception	Western-style
arranged	✔ bachelorette	exchange	performs	vows	

1. Before the wedding, the bride and her female friends have a ___bachelorette___ party.
2. In the same way, the groom and his male friends have a _____ party.
3. The parents of the groom _____ a dinner the evening before the wedding.
4. In some weddings – for example, _____ weddings – the bride and her father walk down the _____ .
5. During the ceremony, the bride and groom _____ rings – often simple gold or silver bands.
6. As the bride and groom give each other the rings, they exchange _____ , promising to love each other forever.
7. Some couples prefer to have a religious wedding; others prefer a _____ .
8. In some weddings, a celebrity look-alike _____ the ceremony.
9. After the wedding, the bride and groom and the guests go to the _____ .
10. People that meet each other through a matchmaker have an _____ marriage.

About you

C Answer the questions with information about typical weddings in your country.

1. What kinds of weddings do people typically have?

_____

_____

2. What kinds of traditions are associated with weddings?

_____

_____

3. Are bachelor and bachelorette parties popular? What other traditions are there before a couple gets married?

_____

_____

Lesson A Grammar Adding information

A Complete the blog post with *when*, *where*, or *whose*. Add commas where necessary.
Sometimes more than one answer is possible.

BLOG

I live in a small town _____ everyone gets married before they're 30, so I have a
lot of friends _____ only ambition is to get married. To me this seems like a waste
of your youth, which is a time _____ you should be enjoying yourself. What's
even worse is that I have some friends _____ parents are almost forcing them
to find a partner. They feel ashamed if they're still single at 30 _____ people say
they're "over the hill" – as if 30 is old! I just think this is a very old-fashioned view, especially
in today's society _____ there are so many opportunities to do other things.
I think it's better to wait and get married in your thirties _____ you know exactly
what you want. I'm sure you get to a point in your life _____ you want to settle
down with one special person. I think, though, you have to make your own choices and not
be persuaded by people _____ own life choices might be different from yours.

B Rewrite each pair of sentences as one sentence, using relative clauses. Replace the words in
bold with *when*, *where*, or *whose*. You may need to change the word order and the punctuation.

1. I'll always remember my best friend's wedding. Nothing went right **there**.

   _____

2. The day before the wedding, we had a rehearsal. **Then** everything went really well.

   _____

3. However, later that evening, the couple was late because their taxi broke down. **Their** parents
   hosted a really expensive dinner.

   _____

4. There was a very funny moment during the ceremony. **At this moment**, the groom got the
   bride's name wrong as he was saying his vows.

   _____

5. The best man left the groom's ring in his car. **His** job was to take care of the rings.

   _____

6. After the ceremony, we all got into cars to go to the hotel. The reception was being held **there**.

   _____

7. The car took me and the other bridesmaids to the wrong hotel, and we didn't realize till the very
   last moment. **That was the moment** we saw the car drive away.

   _____

8. For the newlyweds, the reception was the best time. **Then** everything finally went according to plan.

   _____

About
you

C Complete the sentences to make them true for you. Add commas where necessary.

1. It would be nice to get married in _____ where _____ .

2. A lot of people get married in _____ when _____ .

3. If I get married, I would have a _____ whose job would be to _____ .

Lesson B Grammar Giving things to people

A Unscramble the sentences to complete the conversations.

1. **A** You know what I've just realized? <u>I never gave you a birthday present!</u>
   (a / gave / I / you / never / birthday present!)
   B Yes, you did. Don't you remember? _____ in the mail.
   (a gift card / me / You / sent)

2. **A** _____
   (offer / you / I / something to drink? / Can)
   B Yes, please. _____
   (Could / make / tea / some / you / us? / for)

3. **A** What did your brother get for his birthday? _____ again?
   (a / sweater / Did / for / him / make / your aunt)
   B No. _____ this year.
   (make / one / him / didn't / She)

4. **A** _____
   (Would / blue jacket? / you / me / your / lend)
   B Sure, no problem! Actually, I don't wear it much. _____
   (I'll / it / give / you / to / if you like.)

5. **A** _____ They smell wonderful.
   (flowers? / you / sent / these / Who)
   B _____ out of the blue.
   (them / sent / My girlfriend / to / me)

6. **A** Isn't it your parents' anniversary today? _____
   (Did / get / you / a gift? / them)
   B Yes, it's today. _____ last weekend.
   (one / them / bought / I)

About you

B Rewrite the questions using the alternate pattern where possible. Then write answers that are true for you, using the pronouns *it, them,* or *one.*

1. Would you ever lend your laptop to a friend?
   Q: Would you ever lend a friend your laptop?
   A: Yes, I'd lend it to him. OR: No, I wouldn't lend it to him.

2. When would you give money as a gift to someone?
   Q: _____
   A: _____

3. Did you buy a birthday present for your best friend last year?
   Q: _____
   A: _____

4. If a good friend liked your new, expensive pen, would you give it to him or her?
   Q: _____
   A: _____

5. When you were little, did you use to make your parents cards or gifts?
   Q: _____
   A: _____

Lesson C   Conversation strategies

A   **Match the sentences and the responses. Write the letters a–e.**

1. I never know what gifts to buy for people. _____
2. I always treat myself to something a bit special on my birthday,
   like a new outfit or something. _____
3. You know, I never buy birthday cards. There isn't really any
   point – no one keeps them. _____
4. You know what I hate? They always put seasonal gifts out in the stores months ahead. _____
5. We never wrap gifts. Do you? We just put something in a gift bag. It's so much easier. _____

a. Though kids like to open all the paper and ribbons, and stuff. It's kind of more fun for them.
b. Right. Though it's slightly odd not to get a card. You can always send an e-card, I guess.
c. Which is sort of nice – to spend money on yourself occasionally.
d. I know. I find it kind of difficult to choose the right thing, too.
e. I know. It's not quite right. I'd rather buy stuff a couple of weeks before the actual holiday.

B   **Check (✔) the appropriate response in each conversation.**

1. *A* I think it's kind of fun to share our traditions with people from other cultures.

   B ☐ Yeah, no. It's kind of important for everyone to know about other customs.

      ☐ Yeah, no. There's no point in learning about other cultures.

2. *A* I've gotten birthday punches ever since I was a kid. I sort of look forward to them.

   B ☐ Yeah, no. It's not very nice. I mean, I'd be somewhat upset, too.

      ☐ Yeah, no. It's good to carry on traditions like that – even if they are slightly odd!

3. *A* Traveling teaches you a lot about different cultures. I think everyone should travel more.

   B ☐ Yeah, no. It helps you understand other people, which makes you more tolerant, I think.

      ☐ Yeah, no. It doesn't really educate you at all.

About
you

C   **Complete *A*'s comments with softening expressions. Use at least five different expressions.
Then write your own responses to complete the conversations. If you agree, use *Yeah, no*.**

1. *A* Why do we celebrate birthdays anyway? In some societies, they don't celebrate birthdays.
   I mean, they think it's _____ odd. They just celebrate when you achieve
   something in your life, which is _____ interesting.
   You: _____

2. *A* I hate it when people send me e-cards. I don't know. It just seems _____ right.
   I mean, _____ lazy – like you don't _____ want to make the effort
   to get me a real card.
   You: _____

3. *A* I think it's _____ important when you get married to start your own traditions
   together. It makes your relationship stronger.
   You: _____

4. *A* I always think it's _____ weird – how people celebrate all the different holidays.
   I mean, even if they don't believe in them. It's just _____ strange, you know?
   Like, it's just an excuse to buy presents and stuff.
   You: _____

Lesson D Reading Reverse culture shock

A **Prepare** **What do you think reverse culture shock is? Check (✔) one box below. Then read the article. Was your answer correct?**

☐ It's what happens when you visit another culture and very little surprises you.

☐ It's the difficulty adjusting to your own culture after living in another one.

☐ It's the problems you have when you first experience a different culture.

Are you ready for reverse culture shock?

1   The term *culture shock*, is used to describe the feeling of unease and/or loss you might experience when visiting or living in a country that is not your own. You might have problems being in a place where you don't speak the language and everyday life is quite different from what you're used to. Initially, this reaction – this shock – may be caused by the feeling that the foreign culture is a threat to your own culture and identity.

2   Less well known, however, is the term *reverse culture shock*, which refers to the difficulties someone can experience on the return to their native country after living abroad. Most people accept that culture shock is a normal part of being in a foreign country. However, it is not so widely understood that people coming home after a stay abroad might also experience a similar kind of culture shock. Living in another country changes you: once you're home, you're no longer the same person who left. With global travel becoming more and more popular and more people living abroad for longer periods of time, it is difficult to dismiss reverse culture shock as something that only happens to a handful of people. It is clearly becoming a more common problem.

3   The level of reverse culture shock that people experience varies, depending on factors such as how positive their experience abroad was and how different the other culture was from their own. It is, however, perfectly normal, and is usually experienced in distinct phases.

4   **PHASE 1** You've made the decision to go home after a few months, years, or decades abroad. It is no less of a big step to take than the decision that brought you to the foreign country in the first place. This time you're leaving a country whose culture you worked hard to understand, where you learned to communicate, and where you made a life. You're leaving a lot behind, but you're probably too excited and too busy preparing to think about that.

5   **PHASE 2** Back home again, you're happy to see friends and family, and they're happy to see you. It's almost like being in a new country, but with the added benefit of knowing the language and culture. You can revive relationships with friends and family, and tell them about your experiences. You look for the opportunity to point out how differently people do things in the other culture. In fact, that's all you seem to want to talk about – something that your friends and family might not appreciate.

6   **PHASE 3** At this point, the downside of moving back hits you. You sense that you're always focusing on the differences between your native country and the country you came from and you don't feel good about it. You might also feel that people in your native country don't really understand you. Since you're used to a different culture, you now feel somewhat uncomfortable in your own. At the same time, you want to preserve everything you feel was good about your time abroad and don't want other people or daily life in your native country to kill off those experiences and those memories. Consequently, you might feel homesick for the other country or even want to return there. This is a natural part of reverse culture shock.

7   **PHASE 4** After a few months, you'll focus less on the differences between the countries. What was once most important to you – the preservation of your old way of life in a foreign culture – will become less so. You'll feel comfortable again with your first language, and people will come to accept you, as you will also be able to accept them.

8   As you adjust, things will start to seem normal again. Try to combine the positive aspects of your international experience with the positive aspects of your life at home. Make an effort to meet people and take part in the local culture as much as possible. If you can do that, you will finally put reverse culture shock behind you.

B **Read for main ideas** The article describes four phases of reverse culture shock. Write the number of the phase (1–4) next to each description. There are two extra descriptions.

    a. You'll accept the fact that you are back home. _____

    b. You badly miss your friends and family. _____

    c. You're happy to be going back home. _____

    d. You really miss the foreign country and consider moving back. _____

    e. You re-learn your first language. _____

    f. You're excited to see people you love and share your experiences abroad. _____

C **Check your understanding** Choose the correct option to complete the sentences.

    1. The article suggests that culture shock _____ .

       a. happens to very few people   b. is a misunderstood term   c. is a well-recognized experience

    2. According to the article, reverse culture shock is _____ .

       a. increasing   b. declining   c. about the same as it always was

    3. The article is most useful for people who are going to _____ .

       a. emigrate   b. return home after a period abroad   c. live abroad for a few months

D **Read for detail** Are the sentences true or false? Write T or F. Correct the false sentences.

    1. A lot of people are familiar with the term *reverse culture shock*. _____

    2. Reverse culture shock affects a small number of people. _____

    3. The article describes reverse culture shock as a normal experience. _____

    4. The article states that reverse culture shock can happen after a week's vacation abroad. _____

    5. Friends and family might not be very understanding about the effects of reverse culture shock. _____

    6. Reverse culture shock is something that people can get over. _____

E **Vocabulary in context** Complete the sentences with words from the article that mean the opposite of the words and phrases in bold.

    1. After leaving a foreign culture, many people feel that its **preservation** in their lives is particularly important. They feel a sense of _____ when they move from one culture to another. (para. 1)

    2. It is important to **accept** reverse culture shock as a real problem for people, but some people simply _____ it. (para. 2)

    3. Reverse culture shock is not limited to being a **local** issue in one or two countries. It is becoming a _____ one. (para. 2)

    4. People who return to their native country may need to _____ old friendships. However, they can soon **kill** them **off** by talking too much about their life abroad. (para. 5)

    5. Some people see living in a new culture as a **threat** to their own lifestyle and values. Others see it as an _____ to assess their own culture. (para. 5)

    6. Moving back home has **benefits**, but there is also a _____ . (para. 6)

About you **F** **React** What do you think people would have difficulty adjusting to if they came to live in your country? Give reasons for your answer.

_____

_____

_____

_____

Writing A conclusion to an essay

Essay question

Is reverse culture shock a positive or a negative experience?

A Read the thesis statements and the concluding paragraphs. Which thesis statement was in the introduction to each essay? Write a, b, or c. There is one extra option.

a. It is not possible to say if reverse culture shock is a positive or negative experience, since that depends on the individual experiencing it.

b. Reverse culture shock is a negative experience due to the confusion it creates in a person's mind about his or her own culture.

c. Because it gives people the opportunity to develop their minds in various ways, reverse culture shock is a positive experience overall.

1. ☐ In conclusion, reverse culture shock affects people differently. Consequently, it is difficult to know exactly how the experience will affect a person. Nevertheless, the benefits of travel are great, so people should not avoid travel because of a fear of reverse culture shock.
2. ☐ In summary, although it can be challenging, reverse culture shock brings many benefits. People may become more open-minded and understand others better as a result of the experience. Therefore, instead of being afraid of reverse culture shock, we should see it as an opportunity for growth.

B Read the concluding paragraphs in Exercise A again. Circle the expressions that express causes, effects, and results.

C Complete the sentences with the expressions in the box. Sometimes more than one answer is possible.

as a result of	because	because of	consequently	due to	since	so	therefore

1. Reverse culture shock is not well understood, _____ we need to learn about it.

2. _____ , there should be more information about it for migrants.

3. Our awareness of ourselves increases _____ reverse culture shock.

4. Our understanding of the world changes _____ we see things differently.

5. Reverse culture shock is positive _____ it shows that we have successfully taken on a new way of life in a different culture.

6. _____ reverse culture shock, some people might change for the better.

7. Reverse culture shock is a problem. _____ , we need to help people with it.

D Editing Correct the sentences. There is one error in each sentence.

1. Your friends might get annoyed due to your complaints about your own culture.

2. I am worried about returning home from a year abroad because reverse culture shock.

3. You are going home soon, consequently start catching up on the news of your country.

4. Since reverse culture shock, I learned a lot about myself and my culture.

5. People will not stop traveling just due to their fear of getting reverse culture shock.

E Write a concluding paragraph to answer the essay question. Include two arguments to support your answer. Then check your paragraph for errors.

Listening extra A destination wedding

A Look at the photos. What do you think a "destination wedding" is? Check (✔) a, b, or c.

☐ a. It's a wedding where the couple has never met before, because it's been arranged by a matchmaker.

☐ b. It's a wedding that is held in a location that isn't the bride's or the groom's hometown.

☐ c. It's a civil ceremony that is performed by a government official.

B 🔽 Listen to the conversation. Was your answer in Exercise A correct? Then check (✔) the topics Diana and her friend Atsuko discuss.

☐ Diana's new responsibilities at work

☐ A recent trip Atsuko made

☐ Atsuko's friend's wedding

☐ The health of Diana's family

☐ Buying wedding gifts

☐ The advantages of getting married close to home

C 🔽 Listen again. Circle the correct option to complete each sentence.

1. Diana and Atsuko haven't seen each other for **a few days** / **a long time**.
2. Atsuko was **a bridesmaid** / **a guest** at her friend's wedding.
3. Diana's cousin wanted a **big** / **small** wedding.
4. Atsuko's friend had a **Western-style** / **traditional** wedding.
5. Atsuko cried at the moment when her friend **helped her father down the aisle** / **said her vows**.
6. Atsuko's only complaint was that the trip **cost a lot** / **was too short**.
7. Diana **attended** / **didn't attend** her cousin's wedding.
8. Atsuko **bought** / **didn't buy** a gift for her friend.

About you

D 🔽 Listen again to some of the comments Diana and Atsuko make. Write your own responses. Use *Yeah, no* if you agree.

1. _____

_____

2. _____

_____

3. _____

_____

4. _____

_____

About you

E Answer the questions. Give as much information as you can.

1. Has anyone you know ever had a destination wedding? Are they popular in your country?

_____

_____

2. What do you think about destination weddings? Are they a good idea?

_____

_____

Now complete the *Unit 11 Progress chart* on page 99.   Unit 11: Culture   **89**

Ability

Lesson A Vocabulary Talking about intelligence

A **Complete the sentences with the types of intelligence in the box.**

| bodily | interpersonal | intrapersonal | linguistic | mathematical | musical | spatial |

1. Architects need _____ intelligence so they can design living spaces.
2. Some people can play an instrument well. They have _____ intelligence.
3. People who don't understand others often have no _____ intelligence.
4. People who know themselves and what they want tend to have _____ intelligence.
5. A lot of children have _____ intelligence and learn through play and movement.
6. Computer programmers have _____ intelligence. Many study math.
7. It's easy to confuse _____ intelligence with being generally very smart. Perhaps because it's important to be able to communicate well.

B **Complete the sentences with the words in the box. Sometimes more than one answer is possible.**

adept	capacity	sensitive
articulate	literate	skilled
capable	scientifically minded	talent

1. My dad's so good at math. He's _____ of solving any problem.
2. My friend really has a _____ for music. He can play anything.
3. My brother always seems to find the right words in any situation. He's very _____ .
4. My mom volunteers in a school, teaching kids to read. She says the key to success in life is to be _____ .
5. I'm not at all _____ . I have no idea about physics or chemistry or anything like that.
6. When I have a problem, I always talk to my sister. She's so _____ to everyone's feelings. She has a great _____ for understanding people.
7. I can't fix anything in the house if it breaks. I guess I'm just not _____ at things like that.
8. My friend is very _____ at balancing work and his social life. It's good to be able to do that.

About you

C **Use the expressions in the box to write sentences that are true for you or people you know.**

| be (not very) adept at | be (in)capable of | be (not very) skilled at |
| be (un)able to | be (not very) efficient at | have a/no talent for |

1. _____
2. _____
3. _____
4. _____
5. _____
6. _____

Lesson A Grammar Describing people and things

A Add the adverb form of the adjectives in parentheses to these sentences. Sometimes more than one answer is possible.

1. Singers don't have to be ⌃ technically perfect – they just need to be able to express emotions. (technical)
2. It's important to get a college education to get ahead in life. (extreme)
3. If you are a lawyer, you need to be very articulate to become skilled. (high)
4. I don't believe that some people can speak seven languages – no one can be so gifted. (linguistic)
5. It's interesting to read about different types of minds and intelligences. (incredible)
6. Students who are very musical often do well in math, too. (remarkable)
7. Intrapersonal intelligence is difficult to learn, but it's an important skill. (particular)
8. It's easy to take really good photos with the latest cameras. (relative)

About you

B Rewrite five of the sentences above, either giving your own views or adding more ideas.

I think you also need to have especially good interpersonal skills to be a successful lawyer.

_____

_____

_____

_____

_____

C Complete the blog post with a correct adverb or adjective form of the words given.

BLOG 24 MAY 💬 No comments

I've never really been _____ (mathematical / talented), but I needed math

to graduate from high school. So my mom contacted a friend of hers, Valli, who had been

_____ (particular / good) at math when they were in school together. Valli wasn't

_____ (high / qualified), but she was _____ (extreme / patient)

and gave me _____ (incredible) confidence. You see, she was an elementary

school teacher, so she had a _____ (wonderful) talent for describing and

explaining things _____ (extreme / clear). She started at the beginning with

_____ (basic) principles and we went over everything _____ (slow).

I learned a lot from her _____ (remarkable / quick), and although I still found math

_____ (relative / difficult), I managed to get a passing grade.

About you

D Write sentences about . . .

1. an activity you are relatively skilled at. _____
2. a place that you think is remarkably beautiful. _____
3. something you find physically impossible. _____
4. a subject that you find particularly challenging. _____
5. a piece of news you find incredibly interesting. _____

Lesson B Grammar Comparing

A Complete the conversations with the comparative or superlative form of the adjective or adverb given. Use *less, least, more,* or *most* where necessary.

1. *A* Hey, your English is improving. I mean, you speak a lot _____ (well) and much _____ (confidently) than before.

   B Well, I just took an intensive course. It was _____ (hard) thing I ever did, and I was _____ (bad) student in the class, but it helped.

2. *A* Every time I play my flute, I think I'm playing _____ (badly) than ever.

   B Well, maybe you need to practice _____ (frequently).

   A I know, but finding time is _____ (hard) thing. I'm _____ (busy) now than I ever was.

3. *A* I hate going to discos. I think I must be just about _____ (bad) dancer in the world. It's the one thing I feel _____ (confident) about.

   B Well, come out with me and Katia. Maybe you'll feel _____ (nervous).

   A Thanks. But Katia's _____ (good) dancer I've ever seen. I think it'd make me feel _____ (embarrassed).

4. *A* Hey, you're early! The traffic must have been _____ (good) than usual.

   B Actually, I came on my bike. I can get across town much _____ (quickly) than in my car. It's _____ (easy), too. You don't need to find a parking space.

   A Right. And it keeps you in shape. You look _____ (healthy) than ever!

B Circle the correct option to complete the blog posts.

Q: I sometimes need to give presentations, but I'm not as **confident** / **confidently** as I'd like to be. Is there anything I can do so it becomes **easier** / **more easily**?

A: Why not take a public-speaking class? Then you'll have the chance to practice more **often** / **frequent**, and you'll feel **less** / **least** nervous. Find the best course **in** / **of** your area.

Q: I don't speak Spanish as well **as** / **than** I did when I lived in Spain. Any suggestions?

A: You need to practice **as often as** / **more often** you can. Joining a conversation group is the **best** / **better** way to get the practice you need. It's also **the least** / **less** expensive way.

About you

C Complete *B*'s responses. Then write answers that are true for you.

1. *A* Would you like to be more confident when you speak English?

   B Yes, I'm not as <u>confident as I'd like to be</u> .

2. *A* Is English the hardest class you have ever taken?

   B No, I think math is _____ .

3. *A* Had you hoped to improve your English more quickly?

   B Yes, I feel that I'm not improving _____ .

4. *A* What skill should you practice more often?

   B Probably typing. I don't _____ .

5. *A* What do your friends do better than you?

   B They all drive better. I'm _____ of all my friends.

Q & A BLOG

Lesson C Conversation strategies

A Complete the sentences. Write the letters a–g.

1. My parents bought me a piano _____ , but I still never learned to play well.
2. To succeed, it's not enough to be gifted. You have to be serious, _____ .
3. I don't think it's a good idea for parents to push their children _____ .
4. I have a lot of practical skills, like I can build furniture, _____ .
5. I wish I could write music _____ , but I'm not as creative as I'd like to be.
6. I guess I'm not a very disciplined student. I'm always turning assignments in late _____ .
7. I know this twelve-year-old girl who's amazingly gifted. She already does algebra _____ .

a. or force them to take dance lessons and stuff
b. or write the lyrics for songs and that sort of thing
c. and speaks three languages, and everything
d. and waiting until the last minute to study and stuff
e. work hard, and make good decisions and all
f. and paid for music lessons and all that
g. fix a car or a computer and that kind of thing

B Circle the best option to complete the conversations.

1. *A* **I think I did well on / I'm afraid I failed** my tests this week.
   B Oh, no doubt. You've done all your homework, and you studied hard, so . . .

2. *A* I think my sister **will make a great nurse / will decide not to go into nursing**.
   B I don't doubt it. She's really good at caring for other people.

3. *A* I think speaking in public is **fun / something you have to practice**.
   B Oh, there's no doubt about that. I mean, you can be articulate and all that, but still find it difficult.

C Complete the conversations with vague expressions and expressions like *No doubt*. Don't repeat any expression. Then write your own responses to *A*'s comments.

1. *A* Families don't seem to play board games anymore. You know, like chess, checkers, _____ . It's too bad because kids learn a lot of valuable skills from games like that.
   B Oh, _____ . They say chess is really good for teaching problem solving.
   You: _____

2. *A* All kids should do music and play an instrument _____ . It's good for them.
   B Oh, _____ . They say if you're good at music, you'll be good at math, too.
   You: _____

3. *A* All kids are good with technology because they grow up with computers _____ .
   B Oh, _____ . Yeah, no. They figure out all that stuff early on.
   You: _____

4. *A* I've heard that a lot of students in college aren't capable of producing a well-written essay.
   B _____ . They don't focus enough on spelling and writing _____ .
   You: _____

Lesson D Reading Overcoming dyslexia

A The word *dyslexia* comes from the Greek: *dys* meaning "ill" or "difficult," and *lexis* meaning "word." Which statements do you think are true about people with dyslexia? Check (✔) the boxes.

☐ They have trouble reading, writing, and spelling.
☐ They are lazy in school.
☐ They are often especially intelligent.

☐ They usually never learn to read.
☐ They are not as articulate as other people.

B Read for main ideas Read the article. Which of the statements in Exercise A are true?

Actors with dyslexia: disabled or gifted?

1   Dyslexia is a language-based learning disability that makes reading, writing, and spelling difficult. The experience of being dyslexic can be extremely challenging. People often have preconceived ideas about dyslexic children who cannot keep up in class or who find it difficult to spell or read properly, and they are often labeled "lazy" as a consequence. These students may feel inadequate, lose interest in studying at an early age, and even quit school. Although people with dyslexia are faced with learning challenges from an early age, many are highly intelligent and succeed in a wide range of careers. There are world-champion swimmers, and Formula One racers with dyslexia – but *actors*? Surprisingly, even though actors need to be skilled at reading scripts, as well as adept at learning lines, there are a number of well-known and highly successful actors who have this condition.

Keanu Reeves

2   Actor Keanu Reeves, who is dyslexic, was typical of many dyslexic children whose differences in learning kept him from participating confidently in school. Although talented and intelligent, Reeves never finished high school. Nevertheless, he dedicated his life to acting and has a very successful career, starring in movies like *Speed*, and *The Matrix*.

3   Actors with dyslexia often have to work harder than other actors in order to be successful. Actors have to read and remember many lines of text. While for some, remembering lines is relatively easy, others spend half their lives studying scripts. Orlando Bloom, whose movies include *Lord of the Rings* and *Pirates of the Caribbean*, has said that reading and memorizing his lines is very hard work. Actor Keira Knightley, also dyslexic, said that, when she was growing up, reading was a tremendous challenge for her but that the struggle made her tougher. The star of *Pride and Prejudice* says that she drove herself very hard to overcome dyslexia and finished school with top grades, in spite of her disability.

Orlando Bloom

4   Successful actors with dyslexia challenge our views about disabilities. Conventional wisdom says that dyslexia is a disability. Today, however, some researchers believe that it is actually a natural ability, a talent. They believe that people with dyslexia, if supported and allowed to develop, have higher than normal intelligence and can be more creative. Orlando Bloom looks at dyslexia as a gift, saying that rather than being a disability, it is a challenge that he uses as motivation to have "a big life."

Keira Knightley

5   In conclusion, actors with dyslexia are able to shine a light on the issue of dyslexia. They demonstrate that with courage and hard work, people with dyslexia can use their special talents to succeed in life. These admirable actors can also raise awareness of the issue of dyslexia so that we can better understand, help, and appreciate people who struggle with it.

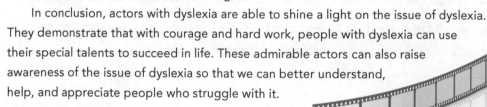

C Understanding viewpoints **Would the writer of the article agree with these views? Write Y (Yes), N (No), or NG (Not Given, if it is impossible to say what the writer thinks).**

1. Being dyslexic can be slightly difficult at times. _____
2. Dyslexic children have a harder time than dyslexic adults. _____
3. Dyslexic people quit school because their problems haven't been understood. _____
4. It's not surprising that dyslexic people go into acting as a career. _____
5. Keanu Reeves lacked confidence at high school. _____
6. Actors with dyslexia can easily overcome their difficulties. _____
7. Dyslexic actors are often more successful than other actors. _____
8. People generally see dyslexia as a disability. _____
9. Dyslexia doesn't have to be seen as a disability. _____
10. Actors with dyslexia spend a lot of time promoting awareness of the condition. _____

D Read for detail **Circle the correct answers to the questions.**

1. Why do dyslexic children sometimes feel inadequate?
   a. They quit school early.
   b. They find lessons difficult.
   c. They have too many preconceived ideas.
   d. They develop few interests.

2. In what way was Keanu Reeves typical of many dyslexic children?
   a. He wanted to be famous.
   b. He became highly successful.
   c. He didn't graduate from high school.
   d. He had a talent for acting.

3. What effect has dyslexia had on Keira Knightley?
   a. It made her difficult to work with.
   b. It made her more intelligent.
   c. It made her successful.
   d. It made her stronger.

4. How do more recent views of dyslexia differ from conventional wisdom?
   a. They see dyslexia as a positive thing.
   b. They say dyslexic people have courage.
   c. They view dyslexia as a disability.
   d. They say dyslexia gives people a better life.

E Focus on vocabulary **Find the words in the article that are used with the words in bold. Then use the words to complete the sentences below.**

1. People often **have** _____ **ideas** about children who have trouble reading. (para. 1)
2. One person with dyslexia became a _____-_____ **swimmer**. (para. 1)
3. Keanu Reeves has _____ his **life** to his acting career. (para. 2)
4. Some actors _____ **half** their **lives** studying scripts. (para. 3)
5. Successful actors _____ our **views** about dyslexia. (para. 4)
6. Although _____ **wisdom** says that dyslexia is a disability, for some it may be a talent. (para. 4)
7. Dyslexic actors _____ **a light** on the issue of dyslexia. (para. 5)
8. Actors like Keanu Reeves, Orlando Bloom, and Keira Knightley _____ **awareness** of the issue of dyslexia. (para. 5)

About you

F React **Answer three of the questions with information that is true for you.**

1. What did you know about dyslexia before you read the article?
2. Did the article affect your view of dyslexia in any way? If so, how?
3. Did the article contain any information that was new or surprising to you? If so, what?
4. Do you feel the article left any information out or got any information wrong? In what way?
5. What else would you like to know about dyslexia?

Writing An essay

Choose three of your most important skills or abilities, and say why they are or will be important in your life. Give specific reasons and details to support your answer.

A Read the beginning of an essay. Underline the three skills or abilities the writer mentions. Then complete the sentences with the expressions in the box.

in order to succeed	so that I don't make	so I can understand	to be

There are three abilities and skills that are important in my life, and that I rely on _____ happy and successful. First, I have an ability to understand other people's feelings. This is one of the main reasons I have a wide circle of friends. Second, I have excellent study skills, which are important _____ in school and work. Third, my ability to understand myself extremely well is a critical skill to have _____ poor choices in life. Together, I believe these three skills will enable me to achieve both success and happiness.

In terms of the first ability, I feel I have a particularly high level of interpersonal intelligence. For example, I am always sensitive to other people's feelings. I listen to people very carefully _____ their points of view. . . .

B Rewrite each pair of sentences as one sentence, using the expressions in parentheses. Make any other necessary changes to the original sentences.

1. When I don't see my friends regularly, I call them. I want to keep in touch. (in order to)
   When I don't see my friends regularly, I call them in order to keep in touch.

2. I often send friends a quick text message. I want to say "good luck" before a test. (to)
   _____

3. I always keep my promises. That way people know they can trust me. (so)
   _____

4. I tend to study on weeknights. Then I have time for my friends on the weekends. (so that)
   _____

5. Every day I set aside some time. That way I can review my notes and assignments. (in order to)
   _____

C Editing Circle the correct option to complete the sentences. In some sentences, both options are correct.

I have not always thought carefully about my life choices, **so / so that** I have made some bad decisions in the past. However, I have tried to learn from my mistakes **so / so that** I can make better choices in future. For example, everyone told me I should be a lawyer, **so / so that** I went to law school. I soon realized that being a lawyer was not in fact what *I* wanted to do, **so / so that** I left after three months in order to study art. It was an important lesson, and it taught me that I should make decisions **so / so that** *I* am happy – not other people!

D Plan and write your essay to answer the essay question. Then check your essay for errors.

Listening extra *A passion for fashion*

A In your opinion, what are the three most important skills and abilities that a fashion designer needs? Check (✔) the boxes. Can you think of other ideas?

He or she needs to . . .

☐ be able to work under pressure.
☐ have a talent for drawing and art.
☐ be capable of taking control and managing people.

☐ be disciplined.
☐ be adept at predicting fashion trends.
☐ have a capacity for understanding others.

B ⬇ Listen to an interview with Maxine Rothman, a fashion designer. Match the people and organizations with what Maxine says about them. Write the letters a–e.

1. Maxine _____
2. Maxine's mother _____
3. The designer in Paris _____
4. The fashion industry _____
5. Maxine's company _____

a. is not always environmentally responsible.
b. lets Maxine promote her ideas.
c. designs clothes for the office.
d. designs clothes for weekends.
e. trains designers to be disciplined.

Maxine

C ⬇ Listen again. Circle the correct option to complete the sentences.

1. As a child, Maxine was particularly interested in **dolls / clothes**.

2. She first learned to create designs **in a fashion house / at home**.

3. Her mother always **pushed / encouraged** her to become a fashion designer.

4. She started her company because she wanted to **have more control / make more money**.

5. She wants everyone to know about her **ethical / disciplined** way of making clothes.

6. Maxine's employees are paid **as much as / more than** workers in the fashion industry.

7. Maxine's company is **incredibly relaxed / environmentally responsible**.

8. The company makes clothes that people **can wear for a long time / throw away each season**.

About you

D Answer the questions with information that is true for you.

1. Do you think that you have any of the skills to be a fashion designer? If so, which ones?

_____

2. Would you like to have a career as a fashion designer? Why or why not?

_____

3. What is your opinion of ethical clothing?

_____

4. Do you try to buy ethical clothing? Why or why not?

_____

Now complete the *Unit 12 Progress chart* on page 101.

Progress charts

Unit 7 Progress chart

Mark the boxes to rate your progress.
☑ I can do it. ☐? I can do it, but have questions. ☐! I need to review it.
I can . . .

	To review, go back to these pages in the Student's Book.
☐ discuss issues in getting along with people and experiences of growing up.	74
☐ use at least 12 phrasal verbs to discuss house rules and roommates.	75
☐ use infinitives and -ing forms to describe experiences.	77
☐ use expressions like *What I'm saying is* and *I mean* to make my meaning clear.	78
☐ use expressions like *I have to say* to show that I want to make a strong point.	79
☐ say at least six conversational expressions quickly.	141
☐ write a thesis statement using *What* clauses to introduce key points.	82

Unit 8 Progress chart

Mark the boxes to rate your progress.
☑ I can do it. ☐? I can do it, but have questions. ☐! I need to review it.
I can . . .

	To review, go back to these pages in the Student's Book.
☐ discuss farming, food, nutrition, and a healthy diet.	84, 86
☐ use the passive to talk about the past, present and future.	85
☐ use complements of at least 10 verbs that describe causes and effects.	87
☐ name at least 12 human body parts and processes.	86
☐ use rhetorical questions to make a point.	88
☐ use *such as, like, take*, and *for instance* to give examples.	89
☐ decide when to say strong or weak forms of prepositions.	141
☐ write about graphs and charts, and use prepositions and approximate numbers.	92

Unit 9 Progress chart

Mark the boxes to rate your progress.
☑ I can do it. ☐? I can do it, but have questions. ☐! I need to review it.
I can . . .

	To review, go back to these pages in the Student's Book.
☐ define and discuss success and happiness and share stories.	94
☐ use the determiners *all, both, each, every, neither none of, no.*	95
☐ use -ing forms as reduced relative clauses, for events and as subjects and objects.	97
☐ remember at least 10 expressions with *get.*	94
☐ use expressions like *As far as (success) is concerned* to focus in on a topic.	98
☐ use expressions like *As far as I'm concerned / can tell* to give and soften opinions.	99
☐ use appropriate stress in conversational expressions.	142
☐ write a paragraph in an essay using expressions like *in addition to*, to add ideas.	102

Unit 10 Progress chart

Mark the boxes to rate your progress. ☑ I can do it. ☑ I can do it, but have questions. ☑ I need to review it. I can . . .	To review, go back to these pages in the Student's Book.
☐ describe travel and vacations and discuss the effects of tourism.	106
☐ use at least 12 adjectives ending -ed and -ing to describe travel experiences.	106
☐ use reported speech to report statements, questions and instructions.	107, 109
☐ use expressions like *so what you're saying is* when drawing conclusions.	110
☐ say *In what way?* to ask for more details about someone's ideas or opinions.	111
☐ say at least 10 words which have silent or reduced vowels.	142
☐ write a survey article and use expressions like *although* to connect clauses.	114

Unit 11 Progress chart

Mark the boxes to rate your progress. ☑ I can do it. ☑ I can do it, but have questions. ☑ I need to review it. I can . . .	To review, go back to these pages in the Student's Book.
☐ talk about weddings, gifts, and traditions and discuss aspects of globalization.	116, 118
☐ use relative clauses with *when, where*, and *whose*.	117
☐ use verbs with two objects to describe giving things to people.	119
☐ remember at least 15 expressions to describe wedding customs.	116
☐ use expressions like *kind of, a little*, and *not really* to soften my comments.	120
☐ use *Yeah, no.* to agree with someone and then make a comment of my own.	121
☐ say consonant groups when one consonant is not pronounced.	143
☐ write a conclusion to an essay and explain cause and effect with *due to*, etc.	124

Unit 12 Progress chart

Mark the boxes to rate your progress. ☑ I can do it. ☑ I can do it, but have questions. ☑ I need to review it. I can . . .	To review, go back to these pages in the Student's Book.
☐ talk about intelligence, skills and abilities and how to develop talents.	126
☐ use adverbs before adjectives to introduce degree, type, opinion, and focus.	127
☐ use *as . . . as* and comparative and superlative adjectives and adverbs.	129
☐ use at least 12 expressions to describe types of intelligence and abilities.	126
☐ use vague expressions like *and all that* when I don't need to be precise.	130
☐ use *No doubt* to show that I strongly agree with someone.	131
☐ use appropriate stress and intonation for new information.	143
☐ write an essay and use expressions like *so that* to explain purpose.	134

Photography credits

Text credits

Corpus

Development of this publication has made use of the Cambridge English Corpus (CEC). The CEC is a computer database of contemporary spoken and written English, which currently stands at over one billion words. It includes British English, American English and other varieties of English. It also includes the Cambridge Learner Corpus, developed in collaboration with the University of Cambridge ESOL Examinations. Cambridge University Press has built up the CEC to provide evidence about language use that helps to produce better language teaching materials.